# CLOSER:

## GOD'S PRESENCE FROM DUST TO DESTINY

# CLOSER:

## GOD'S PRESENCE FROM DUST TO DESTINY

### BY LYDIA BOHI

*Purpose House Publishing*

Pastor Lydia Bohi was born and raised in Kampala, Uganda. She is a wife, mother, author, former nursing aid, and minister of the gospel. She is the founder of Hope and Joy Again foundation, a children's home based in Uganda, which focuses on giving young people a home and safe place to stay while teaching them about Jesus. Together with her husband, they are the senior pastors of Trinity's Love Ministries International based in Switzerland.

Copyright © 2021 Lydia Bohi. All rights reserved.
Published by PurposeHouse Publishing, Columbia, Maryland.
Cover design by PurposeHouse Publishing, all rights reserved.
Printed in the USA

No part of this publication may be reproduced or distributed in any form or by any means, or stored in a database or retrieval system, without the prior written permission of the author. Requests for permission should be emailed to nabalydia@yahoo.co.uk.

ISBN: 978-1-7329549-6-0

Unless otherwise indicated, all scriptural quotations are from the King James Version of the Bible.

Scripture from the Holy Bible: Easy-to-Read Version (ERV), International Edition © 2013, 2016 by Bible League International and used by permission.

Scripture from The Holy Bible, English Standard Version® (ESV®) Copyright © 2001 by Crossway, a publishing ministry of Good News Publishers. All rights reserved.

Scripture from the Message Bible, Copyright © 1993, 1994, 1995, 1996, 2000, 2001, 2002 by Eugene H. Peterson. All rights reserved.

Scripture from New American Standard Bible, Copyright © 1995 by the Lockman Foundation, All rights reserved.

Scripture from the New International Version, Copyright © 1973, 1978, 1984 by Biblica.

# Dedication

To God, thank you for loving me.

For mommy and daddy, I love you and miss you always.

For Birungi, I love you and miss you a lot.

For Buza, I love you and miss you a lot.

To my brothers, I love you guys for always having my back.

To all my children, you are my heart.

Für meine Schwiegereltern, Mam und Paps, herzlichen Dank für eure Liebe und Unterstützung.

To my husband, honey, making you last is just a trick. Thank you for being by my side. Walking with you in this journey called love and life, I am so blessed to do this all with you. I love you babes.

# Contents

Dedication ........................................................................................ v

Acknowledgements ........................................................................ 3

*Section 1: The Early Days Of Uganda* ........................................ 7

Chapter 1: The Good Life: A Love Story ..................................... 9

Chapter 2: The Murder ................................................................ 15

Chapter 3: No More Good Life, But New Life ......................... 21

*Section 2: Faith Rising* ............................................................... 29

Chapter 4: A Message From A Ladybug And A Preacher ...... 31

Chapter 5: Growing In Faith ....................................................... 41

Chapter 6: Out Of Depression Into A Healing Anointing ...... 51

*Section 3: Graduating To The Next Phase* ............................. 67

Chapter 7: More Than Wages ..................................................... 69

Chapter 8: Would You Like Ice Cream? ................................... 75

Chapter 9: A Switzerland Breakup? ........................................... 79

Chapter 10: Marriage: Yays And Nays ...................................... 89

*Section 4: Becoming One: A New Chapter* ............................ 97

Chapter 11: Give Me Your Heart: Loss And Gain .................... 99

Chapter 12: Birthing: Ministry And Children ........................ 109

**Chapter 13: Our God Reigns**........................................................... 115

*Section 5: Ministry* ............................................................................ *125*

**Chapter 14: Present Day: The Miracles Continue**........................ 127

## Acknowledgements

I want to acknowledge everyone that ever helped my mother. God sent several people to assist us, but one person stood in the gap like a father figure. He corrected us and helped us learn to read and write. He wasn't dating my mother or anything, but he cared for us, and I will always be grateful to God for him. He took us as his own children and cared for us. He never made us feel less loved or rejected. We are still in contact today and look up to him for advice. We call him Uncle Kisseka Charles. Thank you for everything and all the love you showed us—and still show us.

I also want to acknowledge my brothers. John, you have been my guard always. Even if I am your older sister, you always protect me. Thank you. I love you with all my heart.

Dre, you have always supported me in everything I do and protected me since we were little till now. You still do, and for that, thank you. I love you with all my heart.

To my pastors and family from TLM, thank you for receiving us and loving us with one heart. We love you.

Gratefully,

*Lydia Bohi*

# Closer: God's Presence from Dust to Destiny

# Section 1: The Early Days Of Uganda

# Chapter 1: The Good Life: A Love Story

*A happy man marries the girl he loves, but a happier man loves the girl he marries. – African proverb*

When you hear the word Africa, you may picture giraffes and safari or deserts, red mud, and heat. You may not envision romance or what society calls "the good life." But the goodness in my life journey began with my parents. Its roots are in the soul-mate kind of love they found for each other in sunny Kampala, Uganda, a city and country situated in East Africa. Uganda is bordered on the north by Sudan and Ethiopia, on the east by Kenya, on the west by the Democratic Republic of Congo, on the southwest by Rwanda and Burundi, and on the south by Tanzania. When my dad found my mom in Uganda, he married the girl he loved and loved the girl he married.

Uganda is where their love story and my life began, and the memories of my early days were formed. Uganda was home. All its sights, sounds, smells, and people are a part of my memories. And mine and my parents' experiences there have shaped my life. It's home to the faith, family, and culture that have made me who I am today.

When I speak of Uganda, I am aware that every culture is different. And in general, in African cultures, open displays of affection and true love were historically limited.

Tradition affected women's role in society, and men sometimes treated their wives more like property than cherished spouses. This was even more true in my parents' era.

Similarly, children were to be seen and not heard, sometimes rarely hearing "I love you" from their parents. However, my parents created a strong, blended family when such success was rare in a traditional African setting. As children, we felt loved because their love was different; it was strong, open, and apparent.

Their love defied the African cultural norms of the day. There was romance, and their togetherness stood out to me even as a child. Even after their deaths, my family members talked of the depth of love my parents had for each other. It was as if they ignored the cultural backdrop of their day. Or perhaps the cultural norms waned in the light of what they felt for each other and became insignificant for them. The norms were like an extra in a movie no one knows while their love took center stage. Unlike many, their affection was open, and their love evident to all around them.

Understanding my early days, my parents' love, and a little of the Ugandan culture is necessary to appreciate the subsequent ironies in my story. Their relationship wasn't the only thing that was different.

Many people associate Africa with poverty and suffering children. But initially, we did not grow up in poverty. My parents were well-off. They owned businesses and houses in Uganda, Kenya, and Tanzania, and they frequently helped their family members financially. We had relatives who lived in our guest houses, and my mother supported my dad in helping his family.

Some women would not be so welcoming—no, not at all. In the culture, most women would try to hold onto what their husband had—both before and especially after he died. The effects of widespread poverty across the nation included competition, jealousy, and desperation within families. It brought out the wickedness in people such that they would do unspeakable things to hold on to the little they had and would seek to harm their own family members who acquired even minimal wealth. Women often only accumulated wealth through their husbands, and their husband's family members could view them as competition for inheritances and wealth. For these reasons, brothers could hate their sister-in-law, and mothers could hate their daughter-in-law. My loving mother didn't know such a fate would befall her. She opened her heart to my dad's family, and for a while, their love story was enviable.

But like everyone else, their relationship had its challenges. Both of my parents had children before meeting each other, but somehow the challenge didn't subtract from their relationship. My dad was divorced when he met my mom and had had children with his former wife. His former wife's bitterness made her extremely cruel. She had forced him to stop having contact with his oldest son. And she would not accept his support, which means the son lacked when it came to things that required additional finances like his education and well-being. She did not allow my dad to have contact with his children or any other family members; she was very controlling.

But that was before my mom—such tactics could not survive after they united. They were the real deal for each other. They met after my dad divorced his former wife and fell in love.

On their first date, my dad took her to the city (to Nairobi) in Kenya for the first time. This was a big deal. When you live in a neighboring county outside the capital city, trips to the city are viewed as sophisticated and expensive, and even more so are trips to a city in another country. He hired a chauffeur just to show her Kenya in one day. How romantic! He went out of his way to impress her and show her that he really loved her. Such gestures were rare in their culture and time.

He demonstrated extreme love for her in good and bad times. During their marriage, she suffered a miscarriage. She was on bed rest and healing at the hospital. And according to the nurses, my dad wasn't allowed to come into her room. He and us kids had to stay out, but she was missing him. He was waiting outside with siblings in the car. Finally, he couldn't take it anymore. He carried the children one by one on his back and sneaked into the hospital just to see her. His actions demonstrated a tenderness, care, and concern that many African husbands did not have or would not have been able to communicate.

And she reciprocated his love in a way that touched the core of who he was. My mom reunited my dad and his oldest son. She welcomed his children and family, acting opposite to the actions of his former wife, who separated him from his children and family. Even before she became a Christian, my mom was a loving, caring person who shaped my character in such a powerful way. Reuniting my dad with his family was just the kind of person that she was. Sadly, little did she know that a family member would be her husband's downfall. Nonetheless, with mom, my dad had met the love of his life, so he settled with her and built a good life.

My mom and cousins always told us stories about my dad and mom. My mom never remarried after my dad passed away, which says a lot. In the culture and time, remarrying would have been the thing to do to ensure she had money or secure her children's welfare. He died when I was just a small child, and my brothers and sister were not much older. But she chose not to remarry and instead weather the storm of being a widow with children to feed and care for in times of need.

Even in death, their love endured. So my parents and their love are what I remember when I hear the word Africa. Perhaps, after hearing a bit more about them, you now understand why. They are the beginning of my story, even though the next chapter takes a rapid turn from love to death.

Amid their soul-mate love, murder emerged. It's a dark appendage to the light that once shined through my dad, but I must share it with you. Its cruelty is part of the early days of my Uganda, and it created a great tension for my family, the tension between love and death, wealth and poverty, trust and betrayal, and affection and abuse. The cords of this tension pull back the curtain on the evil called murder.

# Chapter 2: The Murder

*Maybe that is why you seem to live more vividly in Africa. The drama of life there is amplified by its constant proximity to death. That's what infuses it with tension. It is the essence of its tragedy too. People love harder there. Love is the way that life forgets that it is terminal. Love is life's alibi in the face of death. — Peter Godwin*

Every family has that one person who seemingly can never keep a job but always has the next great, big business idea. If only you, their family member, can invest in them to prove you love them, everything will be alright. Perhaps you are now picturing that person in your family. In our family, step-uncle was that person. My dad's brother lived in our guest house, enjoying my dad's wealth and support. My parents would often employ him in their various businesses, but somehow it would always end badly. He was my dad's older brother. In our culture, that meant he should have been more responsible and the one in a position to take care of my dad—not the other way around. Still, my parents provided a home for him and supported him.

One day, my dad returned from a business trip, and my step-uncle was eager to present his next idea. He wanted my parents to buy him a bus to start a business, but my mother was not convinced. The conversation went something like this.

"I don't think this will work out. A bus will be too expensive. Why don't you start with something smaller like a taxi?" my mother said.

"With all the money you guys have, you want to reduce me to something small?" step-uncle replied.

"We cannot give you the money this time. We are not going to buy you a bus." said dad.

"You will see!" step-uncle said as he got up and stormed out of the room.

Many traditional African men would have resented my mother even being present in such a conversation. But dad respected my mom and her opinion. Even though he loved his brother, he agreed with my mom and made it clear that he would not buy my step-uncle a bus.

From that moment, step-uncle devised an evil plan and waited for the opportune time to execute it. It was dinner time. After the maid had prepared food for daddy, my step-uncle sneaked into the back door and put poison in the food. He pretended as if he had come to say hi and sat down to watch my daddy, his brother, eat poisoned food. What wickedness! But the scripture is true when it declares that "the love of money causes all kinds of evil." (1 Tim. 6:10 ERV) Only evil could cause someone to be so at ease to sit down and watch their own brother eat poisonous food, rejoicing in their heart as they look on.

After dad had eaten, he felt sick, so they took him to the hospital. They did tests and examined him but could not determine what was wrong. Finally, they discovered that he had been poisoned. And what was my step-uncle doing? He was bragging around town that he had taught daddy a lesson. Before this, my step-uncle would always try to flirt with my mom when dad was not around. Perhaps envy pushed him over the brink. He envied everything my dad had and resented having to ask his younger brother for money. My mother saw through him and never trusted him, but daddy was biased because they were brothers.

Because my dad's physical condition worsened from the poison, the family called for a meeting and confronted my step-uncle about what happened. He had been bragging about it, so it was no shock that he admitted what he had done. But the detestable thing is that he had an antidote for the poison but demanded that daddy apologized for disrespecting him by offering him "little" money instead of paying for the bus before giving it to him. Daddy refused to apologize, saying, "I've always helped you and given you everything." In turn, my step-uncle refused to give daddy the antidote, and my dad died. Sadly, there's a high probability that the antidote wouldn't have helped anyway because the poison had progressed. All his organs were spoiled by the poison. But the wickedness of my step-uncle didn't stop there.

My step-uncle tried to come after my mom because she attempted to have him arrested for what he did. He came to my dad's funeral, and mommy had the cops there dressed in normal clothes to arrest him because he had confessed to what he did. My father's parents were dead, and his only surviving family members were my father's siblings and uncle. My father's uncle worked a plan to help my step-uncle escape from the funeral.

After that, my mom tried to look for my step-uncle, but he moved. She looked for about two years, but he kept moving. Finally, he tried to come after her because, as the oldest brother, he felt entitled to whatever money and possessions my father had left.

To his demise, step-uncle died from HIV/AIDs. Worse, before his death, no one in the family wanted him around anymore. He died a bad death and alone. His family didn't even want his body back because they felt what he did to my dad had brought a curse. So he was buried in no man's land with no one to mourn him.

Still, I invited all his children to my wedding because my mom and I had forgiven him after becoming Christians. But even today, his kids are not in the best condition. The passage in 1 Timothy 6:10-11 not only says the love of money causes all kinds of evil but also that "Some people have turned away from what we believe because they want to get more and more money. But they have caused themselves a lot of pain and sorrow." Step-uncle thought he was winning and teaching my dad a lesson, but his evil actions only caused a lot of pain and sorrow for him and his children.

Like Abel's murder, the first murder in the Bible, my dad's murder underscores several lessons.

> At harvest time, Cain brought a gift to the Lord. He brought some of the food that he grew from the ground, but Abel brought some animals from his flock. He chose some of his best sheep and brought the best parts from them. The Lord accepted Abel and his gift. [5] But he did not accept Cain and his offering. Cain was sad because of this, and he became very angry. [6] The Lord asked Cain, "Why are you angry? Why does your face look sad? [7] You know that if you do what is right, I will accept you. But if you don't, sin is ready to attack you. That sin will want to control you, but you must control it." [8] Cain said to his brother Abel, "Let's go out to the field." So they went to the field. Then Cain attacked his brother Abel and killed him. [9] Later, the Lord said to Cain, "Where is your brother Abel?" Cain answered, "I don't know. Is it my job to watch over my brother?" [10-11] Then the Lord said, "What

have you done? You killed your brother and the ground opened up to take his blood from your hands. Now his blood is shouting to me from the ground. So you will be cursed from this ground. [12] Now when you work the soil, the ground will not help your plants grow. You will not have a home in this land. You will wander from place to place." (Genesis 4:3-12 ERV)

God would have accepted Cain if he had only done well. Abel was innocent and became a target of evil simply because he had found favor and acceptance in God's eyes. Just as Cain reaped consequences for his envy and act of murder, my step-uncle also reaped consequences. And they didn't only affect my step-uncle but also his children. We must all remember that whatever we sow, we reap, and godliness with contentment is great gain. We need not envy or covet what our brother has, but look unto Jesus, the author and finisher of our faith.

And looking unto Jesus, among other things, is what my family learned in the next chapter of our lives. My mom was now a widow. Life changed drastically, and evil continued to attack us through family members. At a time when we should have been given space to mourn, they came to accuse and pillage. It seemed as though the good life was over.

# Chapter 3: No More Good Life, But New Life

> *When the righteous cry for help, the LORD hears and delivers them out of all their troubles. The LORD is near to the brokenhearted and saves the crushed in spirit. Many are the afflictions of the righteous, but the LORD delivers him out of them all. He keeps all his bones; not one of them is broken.*
> *(Psalm 34:17-20 ESV)*

Murderer! That's hardly the accusation you want to hear as a new widow with young children to feed. Even though my dad had left a will and testament that everything he owned should be left to my mom and us, his family accused my mother of killing him herself to steal his money. They were present when my step-uncle confessed, but accusing my mother was their excuse to pillage everything we had. And they took everything! Suddenly, the good life was over.

It was as if my mother had no time to mourn. The moment they found out that daddy had stopped breathing, they stormed into our home and started packing things, including forks, knives, and anything they could put their hands on. They were like vultures released on fresh meat. They touted that the things had belonged to their brother, and therefore, they were entitled to them, and my mother was just a woman and entitled to nothing. Mom was left without a penny or possession and nowhere to start. My dad's family even sold our property and lands. What selfishness; there was no care or concern for how we kids would survive. Although she was a grown woman with kids, she had been stripped of everything she and my dad had built together. Without my dad to defend her, my mom had no choice but to return to her parents to survive.

My grandparents (my mom's parents) had their own properties. They used to have a nightclub that wasn't operating anymore, so they told mom she could move in there. It was a hard transition for my siblings and me. My mom used to comment about how we were so used to the upper lifestyle and lament that the only thing she could afford to give us was tea without sugar. There was no bread and no milk—you just had to survive. My brother cried a lot because he had gotten used to a lifestyle my mom could no longer provide. Why was daddy gone? Why was all this happening to us? Why did life have to change, we wondered.

Why had we been stripped of our father, the good life we once had, and why was there no hope in sight for our future? How does a child process all these questions? We went from having guest houses to living in the slums of Uganda, much like the slums you see in the movie, *The Queen of Katwe*. My mom did what she could. For a while, she went back into the import and export business, doing things to try to take care of us. She could have sought out a sugar daddy or married again to secure her station in life, but she never did. She tried to find her own way to take care of us, doing business and taking help from family members here and there to watch us kids. Not only had we lost our dad, but also my mom now had to be away a lot. It was as if life had robbed us of both parents.

For one business trip, mom had to travel to Rwanda and left just a few weeks before the genocide broke out. In total, she would be away for four months. While there, she had a dream. In the dream, I said to her, "Mommy, I've been knocked by a car and fell down." She was very disturbed after having that dream and told those around her something was wrong because she had a dream about her daughter, and she must go home. Two weeks after she left Rwanda, the genocide broke out, and a lot of those she had been within Rwanda died.

Again we saw the tension between love and death. My mom left Rwanda because of her love for me, having been disturbed by a dream, but many she knew died. A few of her friends narrowly escaped with their lives. The Rwandan genocide broke out on April 7, 1994. Two weeks prior, my mom had left what would become one of the bloodiest events in the history of mankind. Still, she died her own kind of death because she came back to Uganda with nothing. Life got worse because she lost her business. And although she didn't die a physical death, something in her changed. She must have taken the loss extremely hard because she started drinking after her return.

> *Its [murder's] cruelty is part of the early days of my Uganda, and it created a great tension for my family, the tension between love and death, wealth and poverty, trust and betrayal, and affection and abuse.*

Was this mom? Well, the hardship had caused depression to set in. I shared a room with my mom divided by curtains. One night, I woke up and heard someone weeping. I discovered it was my mother. She was weeping because she didn't know how she was going to feed us the next day. It's a mother's worst nightmare, and as a child, it was heartbreaking to see my mother in such a state.

Mom had some friends in the village; they would go and drink and come back in the night. But after you drink and the alcohol subsides, reality kicks in. You can't sleep; you are left with only your thoughts and burdens. That is when mom would find herself weeping. During that time, seeing my mother like that felt like sorrow had broken down our front door and moved in, and my mother was defenseless to evict it.

Our challenges were not just emotional. There were other illegal tenants we were battling, namely rats. It was the tension between wealth and poverty, memories of our old life still playing in our minds. Sometimes we would wake up, and the rats had eaten our shoes, clothes, fingertips, and toes. As children, we would eat on the ground in the house. The table was for guests. At one dinner, my brother and I were eating on the ground. My brother was kneeling and eating his food by hand, and out of nowhere, a mouse came and crawled up his shirt. He started yelling and screaming. The next thing I knew, my mother ran across the room and jumped on a chair. As my brother cried, my mother screamed! It was quite a chaotic scene.

Note, we had traps and poison for the rats, but there was one rat that even the cat was scared to attack. You can imagine its size. The rat had staked its claim, and the cat was not willing to challenge it. One night, I was praying earnestly, and afterward, I had a dream that a rat had died. It's an unusual subject matter for a dream. However, we woke up the next morning and discovered that the rat that the cat had been afraid to attack had died in the sitting room. My siblings and I all laugh about it now, but the hardships we had were really challenging. The things we survived as children are simply amazing.

There was one time we hadn't eaten, and we were sitting outside. A guy was walking and holding a lot of bread in a plastic bag. It fell out of his hands and scattered on the ground. So he just picked up "the good bread" and walked off, leaving the rest. We ran to the street and picked up all the bread he left, cleaned it off, and walked home with it. We didn't see it as bad bread; God had provided. We scrubbed off the dust and were happy, giving thanks to God. We even had it the next morning.

Then there was my mother's friend who owned a restaurant (chop shop). She used to collect leftover food from people's plates, and whenever we came and hadn't had anything to eat, she would give it to us after she finished working. We would take it home, pick out the bones, organize them, and eat. We gave thanks for it. When you focus on God alone, he makes even the rags look beautiful to you. I will always be thankful for that woman. Sometimes, I would go to her shop, carrying my brother on my back, and she would give us leftovers. She was not a believer, by the way, but mom tried to preach to her.

Whether mommy was away or around, we used to do domestic work, beg, or just do tasks for food. We would wash clothes, clean houses, and do hard labor. It was not easy washing people's clothes; they were careless and mean. There was this one lady that loved to put her bloody menses underwear in the laundry we would do for her. What could we say? We were vulnerable and needed the money to eat. We just had to wash it—by hand. It was disgusting. My mother's emotional state and our lives had hit rock bottom.

Then, one day mom did something out of the ordinary. She took us to church. Miraculously, we all gave our lives to Jesus that day—all of us. It was no normal occurrence, a mother and all her children accepting Jesus into their hearts in the same service, at the same time—all convinced and convicted of the lordship of Jesus Christ. It's as if God was waiting for the exact right moment. All the affliction and hardship had somehow brought us to the point where our hearts were open. We were ready for change, and the Lord stepped in, prompting our mom to take us to church at just the right time. In the natural, we were crying out to survive, but our spirits were crying out, "What must I do to be saved?"

> And brought them out, and said, Sirs, what must I do to be saved? [31] And they said, Believe on the Lord Jesus Christ, and thou shalt be saved, and thy house. [32] And they spake unto him the word of the Lord, and to all that were in his house. [33] And he took them the same hour of the night, and washed their stripes; and was baptized, he and all his, straightway. (Acts 16:30-33 KJV)

Our entire house was saved that Sunday, and my mother's faith and passion for the Lord began to grow quickly. This was a woman who had been in despair, drinking to drown out her sorrows. But her fire and excitement for Jesus grew strong, and as a result, she made moves that pleased the Lord but upset others. She burned all the indigenous ritual stuff she had. In Uganda and other African cultures, families often adhere to traditional, indigenous religions. And sometimes, each family has its own god or practices ritual worship and sacrifices to their ancestors. If you break from that worship, your family will often fear that you will upset the ancestors or traditional gods and cause problems for the entire family.

With her new faith and conviction, my mom told her entire family of her newfound faith in the Lord, Jesus Christ. My grandparents were not happy; they thought she had lost her mind. And my grandfather threatened to disown her if she didn't renounce Jesus. But the change in her was real. She stopped drinking and put her life in order. The good life of guest houses and wealth was gone, but our family had found new life in Christ.

> *It is good for me that I was afflicted, that I might learn your statutes. (Psalm 119:71 ESV)*

Hallelujah! Only God can change someone from the inside out the way he changed my mom, my siblings, and me. At the time, we were experiencing hardships with no good life in sight, but becoming a Christian does not mean you will never have challenges in life. It does mean you will have the strength of a relationship with your creator and heavenly Father and his promises to bring you through whatever you face.

So my story continued, and everything did not suddenly turn perfect for me. But our family had found new life. We were strengthened by our newly found faith. God walked with me and used one of my most painful secrets to grow my faith. He used a message from a ladybug to give me hope amid a shame I have previously only shared with my husband. I share it with you in the next chapter.

# Section 2: Faith Rising

# Chapter 4: A Message From A Ladybug And A Preacher

> *Please put the ladybug outside without harming her.*
> *(to his butler) – Winston Churchill*

Africa has the largest number of child laborers on the planet, with the youngest laborers, aged 5-11 years old, comprising the largest percentage of child laborers.[1] My siblings and I were among them. If you understand my story, you can understand why this number is so high. Like too many other children, my siblings and I did what we had to do to survive, and my mom had to be away often, trying to find work to be able to feed us. That meant we frequently stayed with family members, which didn't make our plight better. It made it worse.

My aunt scammed my mom. When we stayed with her, she would keep the food mommy would send for us for herself and her son. She never took care of us—never. I took care of my brother. We commonly cooked outside in the dark, with no electricity, but they would enjoy the food. My aunt would receive things for us but not give them to us. Again, she never took care of us. By today's standards, it was outright neglect.

---

[1] "Child Labour in Africa," International Labor Organization (ILO), accessed December 18, 2020. https://www.ilo.org/ipec/Regionsandcountries/Africa/WCMS_618949/lang--en/index.htm.

Strangely, my aunt, uncle, and so many like them had a different standard. For them, children were chattel. They were a means to acquire more for themselves and a mere possession to be bartered or leveraged to fulfill their own greed and lust. Even the cruelest people do not step on a ladybug for admiration of its distinction. My aunt and uncle were the kinds of people who would treat a dog better than they treated us, taking advantage of vulnerable, innocent children. Not only did my aunt neglect us, but also my uncle abused me in a way that could have ruined me for life.

He abused me sexually; once, he made me touch his genitals. This happens a lot in Africa because the children are not protected. I was young, and I never understood why and what it was about. As a kid, you don't know anything sexual or understand anything about arousal. You don't understand what's happening. I felt crippled and as if I couldn't move or scream. I was scared and confused while he was instructing me to touch his genitals. At the same time, I felt disgusted and sick. I didn't like it or want any of the things he was saying or making me do.

My older brother rescued me. He started looking for me because we had been playing outside together when my uncle pretended to ask me to go into grandma's house where he lived to get him a glass of water. As I entered the house, he immediately jumped behind me, locked the door, and started to force me to touch his penis. My brother got suspicious and started yelling my name. He knocked on the door. Then I yelled, "I am here!" My uncle had no choice but to let me go, and my brother knew what had happened. He wanted to fight our uncle, but grandma said, "Keep it quiet. Think about it. When this gets out, people will know about it and talk." My mummy said she was taking him to the police, but again grandma said, "Please don't report him; he will be sentenced." Some years back, my uncle had somehow gone insane. So grandma always used this excuse for him. Every time he did something bad, she protected him. I must have been eight or nine years old when it happened because it was before my first menses.

Unfortunately, that was not my only encounter with such calamity. My cousin's brother-in-law sexually abused me twice. When my cousin sent us outside to cook at night, he would molest me. There was no electricity. I was just alone in the dark, where he made me do all these things. He never penetrated me; I don't know why, but God just saved me from that. However, what he did affected me when I got married. It affected my ability to be intimate with my husband.

I couldn't tell anyone. I feared that if I said anything, I would be sent back home, and mommy couldn't really afford to look after me. Also, I would not have the chance to go to school there. Up until today, no one in my family knows about this. I only shared this with my husband.

The days living with my aunt and uncle were a living hell. Any adult would have sought a place to escape, much more children trying to cope with issues they should never have experienced. When I went outside to my aunt's garden, I would see a lot of ladybugs. There was this theory that you could give a ladybug a message, and it would fly and send the message to whoever you wanted. When I was sad and would see a ladybug in the garden, I would tell it, "Please tell mommy to come and get me."

I didn't know that the theory about ladybug's being special messengers went as far back as the days of King Robert II in France. A French folklore tale describes the execution of a criminal who was ordered to be beheaded by King Robert II of France. When the convicted criminal laid his head on the executioner's block, a ladybug settled on his neck. During this era, ladybugs were thought to be good luck and a symbol of the divine related to the Virgin Mary. So the executioner stayed his hand at the sight of the ladybug and gently removed the bug from the criminal's neck. The ladybug persisted and continued to land on the prisoner's neck each time the executioner tried to land his ax. When King Robert II saw this, he declared it a sign of divine intervention and stopped the execution. Days after, the real perpetrator of the crime was captured and confessed. The ladybug had saved an innocent man's life.

My innocence had been victimized, but somehow it seems God heard the message I was sending my mom through the ladybug because my oldest brother came to check on us. When he arrived, I told him I wanted to come home. He saw how my baby brother had been bitten by mosquitoes and was malnourished. I'm sure he could see that we were both looking neglected because although my aunt protested, my big brother took us without her permission. My baby brother looked like he had a rash because of all the mosquito bites. When we arrived home, mommy couldn't believe how we looked.

Finally, we were rescued and back home with my mom, but the drama didn't stop. One day, my cousin's ex-girlfriend came with a baby to visit at my grandmother's shop. (He wasn't a close cousin. He was my grandmother's nephew.) I used to help my grandmother with errands and serving customers. That day, I was the only one there. And I was an easy target because I was young, and I loved children. I didn't ask her too many questions. The baby was about three months old, and he had a lot of spots all over his body. I didn't know it at the time, but these were symptoms of HIV/AIDS. At that time, AIDS was an epidemic in Uganda, and there was not adequate treatment.

My cousin's girlfriend said I should look after the baby while she went to the toilet. Two or three hours later, grandmother realized that she had run off and abandoned the baby. I was so terrified because I didn't know how my mom was going to react. The lady had left the baby with me without my mom's permission, and I felt responsible for it. I loved children, but I knew she already had so much pressure on her. After about three hours, my mom sent my big brother to get me because I didn't show up for lunch. I was in tears when he arrived, crying because I was thinking my mom was going to give me a whipping.

I was shocked when mom said it was okay and took the baby out of my arms. Mom said we'd have to find a way to contact the father. We found out that that cousin of mine was HIV positive. That's probably why his girlfriend abandoned the baby. Grandmother sent someone to the village. They got the father to come to the city, and he took his son. I never found out what happened to the baby. This incident, along with my own challenges as a child, fueled my love for children.

My compassion for children started at an early age. I always felt that later in life, when I had the money, I wanted to have a children's ministry that would give needy children a home and a family—a place to feel safe. God, the heavenly Father, was working in me his love, the kind of love that protects children who cannot protect themselves. Little did I know, I would become his arms and hands, extending compassion to children who would go through some of the very things I suffered as a child. This is our heavenly father's heart. Unlike my aunt and uncle, children are not chattel to him; they are precious in his sight. And he extends his arms and hands to bless them.

> And they were bringing children to Him so that He might touch them; but the disciples rebuked them. But when Jesus saw this, He was indignant and said to them, "Permit the children to come to Me; do not hinder them; for the kingdom of God belongs to such as these. Truly I say to you, whoever does not receive the kingdom of God like a child will not enter it at all." And He took them in His arms and began blessing them, laying His hands on them.
> (Mark 10:13–16 NASB)

Glimpses of joy started to shine in our lives. We started volunteering in the church canteen. I loved working in the canteen so much, but not necessarily the cleaning part. Because we had to clean after everyone had gone, we used to be the last people to leave the church. My love for God started there, but I enjoyed going to adult church more than spending time in children's Sunday school.

My younger brother, cousin, and cousin's sister played church after everyone left the building. I was always the preacher, and my cousin was the praise and worship leader. Our favorite song to sing in our pretend service was *When I Reach Heaven*. We imagined that the things we couldn't afford to have were free in heaven. After singing, they would invite the preacher. "Let's invite Leanny," they would say. But I was extremely shy in those days. My mom used to say, "If you want to start preaching, you have to start talking to empty chairs to get over your shyness. If you want to be a preacher, you have to talk to these chairs." I used to stand on a crate in the canteen as a podium because I was so short.

We were poor, but the Lord had come into our lives. There was something different. My mother would tell us, "He's a father to the fatherless and a mother to the motherless. If you need anything, just tell him." That's the kind of relationship she had with him, and in that time with mom, she taught us to rely and depend on God.

One night, mommy called a family meeting. Easter was coming, and we had been without food in the house for a while. We used to pray in the morning, at lunch, and before bed. We had our own church in the house as a family. In the meeting, she shared that she only had 1,000 Ugandan Shillings, which is about $1; but we had a heavenly Father. She said, "We're going to talk to God and tell him what we need." Each of us found a place in the house to pray. One sat in the corner, one laid down, and we talked to God. I remember what I prayed. I said to the Lord, "Jesus, we don't have food. We need matoke, Irish potatoes, rice, onions, potatoes, and cooking oil." I made a list for God. I said, "Thank you, Mukama Taata, because I know you hear, and this is what I need." Mukama Taata is Luganda for Father Lord, and it's how we addressed God in the family. Luganda is a Bantu language that over ten million people in Uganda speak. After praying, mommy said, "Now let's wait. We've told him."

In Uganda, we cook outside. So while we were still very hungry and waiting, our neighbors were busy cooking outside, firing up various spices. Mom called us back in the house because, as kids, it was hard to bear. Ten or twenty minutes later, someone knocked on the door. "Somebody get the door," mom said. I went to open the door, and this huge guy who used to work for my parents as a driver for one of their taxis was standing there. "Is mommy home? As I was coming from a work trip, I felt I should bring you this food and other things," he said.

With joy, mommy said, "You guys go out and get the things from the car." From that day on, I learned that those who trust in the Lord and wait on God cannot be disappointed. He had brought everything I had prayed for and even extra things. The gentleman even gave my mom extra cash, pocket money to take us out. I ran into the boys' bedroom, and I knelt down and said, "Thank you. The things are here." There was chicken to be slaughtered, fresh fish, bread, milk, eggs—everything! We had a wonderful Easter.

Not only that, but the gentleman started coming every three or four months to bring us food. He would also add in money for school fees here and there. God had answered us and done exceedingly more than we had asked. The gentleman said my parents had treated him so good and he wanted to repay them. God put it on his heart to remember them and do something kind. It was such a faith booster!

God continued to build our faith, but this time it would be through something painful. After that, mom got breast cancer. She started getting sick and having pain in her breast. There was a discharge. But there was no cancer treatment at that time. We only had access to a doctor in a small village. He helped everyone and did his best to help mommy manage the pain. Her breast got so swollen, and she couldn't afford to go to the hospital.

I was still sharing a room with mommy, separated by a curtain. One night, I walked in with a lantern, and mommy looked up into my eyes. I thought she was dying. So I dropped the lantern and ran to my grandma. Grandma said we should go in and see whether mommy was dead; we were both shaking. "Mama, mama, are you okay?" grandma called out. Mommy looked around and said, "That one is crazy." She was speaking of my reaction. Mommy wasn't dead; I had been afraid and burst into tears. I felt a mixture of sadness about her condition and relief that she was alive.

That following Sunday, we went to church. The pastor gave a word of knowledge, saying, "Someone has breast cancer, and God wants to heal you. Unless this person comes out, I'm not going to preach." We were all looking and saying, "Mommy, it's you, go up front." After hesitating for a while, she finally went to the front. He prayed for her, and right then and there, the bleeding and puss stopped. My mother never had problems with her breast again.

God's hand was moving for us. Our faith was increasing, and although we were not rich, we were encouraged to believe God and serve him with all our hearts. He is truly Mukama Taata, a good, good heavenly Father.

> LORD *my God, I prayed to you, and you healed me.*
> *(Psalm 30:2 KJV)*

My mother continued to grow spiritually. God had healed her of breast cancer, but there were more adventures in store. And in the next chapter, you will learn of a police shootout experience she had while witnessing and sharing Christ with a bank security guard.

# Chapter 5: Growing In Faith

*Bullets were firing. Everyone was running for cover.*

Mom was healed from breast cancer, but out of nowhere, my little brother got shot. My mom was on fire for God and used to go out evangelizing. Even at the bank, she would witness to the security guards. But on this trip to the bank, no one knew there would be a robbery. While there, she said hi to the bank's security guards and began to talk to them about Jesus. One of the guards said, "I really hate God. If you showed me where God is, I would shoot him right now." Another guard reacted, "What did you say? Don't talk like that about God."

Just then, suddenly, the thieves started shooting. My mom was holding my baby brother on her hip. They shot the security guards and went on exchanging bullets for about ten minutes. The guard who said he would shoot God was shot three times by the thieves. He survived but was crippled and became handicapped. The guard who said don't talk like that about God did not get a single scratch.

My mom was hiding in the next shop and saw blood on her clothing. She checked herself and had no wounds. Then she checked my little brother and saw that he had been shot. He didn't scream or anything; she just felt him grab onto her tightly throughout the ten minutes. It was a clean wound; it did not break a bone or damage anything. That was a miracle. My brother was taken to the hospital, and three days later, he went home. It was like nothing happened. It was everywhere in the news, and people came to interview my mother.

Three months later, my mother was walking in the city and happened to meet the guard that said he would shoot God. She asked, "Would you still shoot God?" He replied, "I don't want to talk anything about your God. You already got me into trouble." He had to retire because he was crippled. My faith grew after seeing God's hand move like that.

My mother used to wake us up early in the morning to pray. She used to say, "Three o'clock in the morning is when God is not so busy. You have to wake up early to talk to God." She would say, "Walk around in the house, so you don't fall asleep. Put your feet in cold water and tell God everything you want." She used to tell us, "Tell God now about the spouse you want to marry. It doesn't matter that you are young." So I used to tell God about the kind of spouse I wanted even before puberty.

> *I used to tell God about the kind of spouse I wanted even before puberty.*

She looked for charity organizations that could help young people get an education. I was in *Feed the Children*, for which actor Roger Moore was an ambassador. They paid part of my primary school fees and would send donations of clothes, shoes, books, etc. But the people who worked there in Uganda would first pick out the clothes they wanted for their families. They gave me an XXXL t-shirt, the last thing remaining, which no one in my family could wear because it was so big. You had to take a picture wearing it for the donors and send a letter saying you were happy with the things you received. For me, it was sad. So I decided that when I grew up, I would help children.

From an early age, I started collecting things for children. My mom and I would supply children in the slums, especially at Christmas. During that time, she would let us invite anyone we wanted to Christmas dinner.

Somehow, God always made it possible for us to have food for Christmas, and I mean every food we wanted for Christmas. At other times, I would go to the market to ask vendors for leftovers; you had to be nice to the sellers so they could give you the food they couldn't sell that day. We used to get sweet potatoes, fish bones, and other things people didn't want. My mom always encouraged us to be grateful.

For Christmas, I liked to invite people who had nothing or who were homeless. Whether they were poorly dressed or smelled, she welcomed them. She was a true believer. Christmases were memorable times of God's provision and helping others in need.

There were always memorable occasions in my family. My baby brother was very stubborn, and one day he was playing outside. We had neighbors that had a little garden in which they had planted chilis. He was playing with some of our nieces and neighbors' kids. We were inside washing clothes, having our laundry day.

I don't know why, but my little brother had this idea to pull up the chilis from our neighbor's garden. He just got this idea to rub chilis on the kids' eyes. He was about five or six years old. Out of nowhere, we heard the kids screaming. I was terribly upset; he ran off laughing.

After the kids had calmed down and we washed all their faces, he forgot and touched his own eyes while he was busy laughing at the other kids. He was rolling and screaming and begging anyone to take him inside to do something and help him. He got a taste of his own medicine. This is the same brother who got shot—the baby brother.

In between these crazy moments, God continued to grow my faith. My mother would take jobs here and there but didn't have a stable income. We were now born again but still living with relatives from time to time.

Sometime around 1997, I started getting sick with fever and stomach pain, something like the stomach flu. My mom took me to the village doctor we had. He checked and said everything would be okay. But a week later, I was still sick, especially when I got my menses.

I was terribly ill, and my temperature was high. The doctor gave me malaria medicine, but nothing was working. It went on until I finished primary school, and it increased; I got sicker and sicker. I finished primary school in 2000 and joined high school. I was afraid I wouldn't be able to enter high school because completing primary school was a miracle with all that was going on. I remember I hadn't been going to school for a long time because mommy couldn't pay school fees. But somebody gave us money so I could go to school.

The night before I was to start school, I had been up several times feeling sick. We used this flask to warm water so that in the morning, I could have some breakfast. The flask exploded! I felt so discouraged and wondered, "My goodness, what is this that's following me?" I was so upset; I broke down and cried. Mommy tried to console me. "I'll wake up early and light a fire," she said. I knew she would have to go through a lot. As a kid, I felt so disappointed and questioned why things could not move on. But I ended up going to school, and later someone gave us a flask. This was really a sad memory for me—how poor we were that we couldn't even replace a thermos flask.

The poverty we experienced while I was in primary school made me doubt how I would be able to go to high school. But God touched someone to give me a scholarship for the first term of high school. My uniform and everything was paid for; it was a faith builder. I joined high school like the rest of my classmates, and God paid my school fees.

During that time, I was sick on and off, and the sickness became worse than when I was in primary school. I became closer to God. I joined the Scripture Union in my high school, and we would go out to share with the rest of the students in my school. I would stay back just to talk with God; my relationship with him grew deeper.

One evening I was praying in the back of the classroom. Two girls, Maria and another girl, were in the front talking. Maria told the other girl how terrified she was because she would have an operation to remove one of her kidneys. She spoke of how scared and sick she was. I listened, and I felt so sorry for her.

I went up front to ask, and she explained that she was born with two kidneys, but one never developed. It never grew; it was just there dormant. The doctors wanted to remove the kidney because they believed it was affecting the rest of her body. She had a yellowish color; she didn't look healthy at all.

The health system in Africa is different. So many people die when they go for surgery; it's a scary thing. I told her I was a believer and asked if I could pray for her. So I laid my hands on Maria and prayed for her right in the classroom. I told my mom, and she agreed to wake me up at 3 a.m. every morning to pray for Maria.

Maria wasn't born again; she was Catholic, and her father wanted her to become a nun. Sometime later, she came looking for me at school and gave me a testimony. "You will not believe what happened!" She explained that they prepped her for the operation; her family was there to say their goodbyes. And the surgeon said he wanted to examine her kidneys one more time before they did the surgery. After examining her, the doctor said," I don't believe this! I can't explain it because it looks like both your kidneys are functioning! We have to stop the surgery and do more tests!" Both her kidneys were renewed like nothing had ever happened.

She told her family and the doctor that there was this girl at school, a born-again Christian, who prayed for her. She told them, "I think I have been healed." After telling me what happened, she was thanking me. Because of the miracle that happened, her father told her, "You won't be becoming a nun." She was now healthy and started enjoying life. Unfortunately, she got pregnant and dropped out of school. That experience built my faith, and Maria having to drop out of school taught me not to neglect the grace of God that is extended to us. I was just a teenager, and if I could pray and God healed someone miraculously, then God was truly awesome.

I continued to draw closer to him. There were times I prayed and worshipped, and I was so terrified that any minute I opened my eyes, Jesus was going to be standing right in front of me. I would die (no one can see God and live). The presence of God would be so evident in the room; it overwhelmed me. In my second year of high school, I got stronger in faith, sharing God, and preaching the gospel. But things were still not perfect. Sometimes we had to clean off spoiled potatoes to eat the remaining part.

When my parents had money, they helped a lot of people on both sides of the family. One of them was my uncle from my mom's side. My parents paid for a wedding for him because he couldn't afford it.

After my dad passed away, that uncle lived on the other side of the nightclub we lived in. We were neighbors, sharing the same bathroom, etc. He was very mean and abusive. He called us orphans and other choice names. "You have no share here. You are vagabonds," he would say. But this is someone my parents took care of when he needed them most. At times he would lock the bathroom and refuse to let us use the toilet. He used to sneak and cut our clothes wires (for hanging clothes outside).

He wanted us to leave the property. He was the maternal son of my grandparents and felt we would take over the property, but we just wanted shelter. One time he attacked my younger brother with a machete. My brother still has scars. That was six months after my mom passed away in November 2009. But my brother was still living on the property. He went to use the bathroom in the night, and my uncle attacked him (waiting in the dark for him in the night).

"You don't count because you are children from a daughter. Only children from males are counted important," he would tell my siblings and me. In the tradition, children of a female belong to the husband's (father's) side, so they don't profit the family. When my mom passed away, he would say we were no longer useful because the only thing connecting us to them was gone.

My mom also looked after her sisters before my dad died. She gave them startup money for their businesses. Once, one of them told her to come to her shop, and she would give her money. The moment my aunt saw us coming, her face literally changed. She got so upset as if we had done something wrong, but she had told us to come. She started yelling and told us to sit at the side. Lunchtime came; we spent the whole day waiting, and at the end of the day, she said sorry, the business was not good today. I can't help. So we walked home with no money and no food. I was with my mother that day.

My auntie's husband was very mean. When he would call you, he would refer to you as a fish. We had to eat away from the family with the maid in the other room. No one deserves to be treated like that, especially family. But the scripture is true; it was another trial that would grow my faith.

> In all this you greatly rejoice, though now for a little while you may have had to suffer grief in all kinds of trials. [7] These have come so that the proven genuineness of your faith—of greater worth than gold, which perishes even though refined by fire—may result in praise, glory, and honor when Jesus Christ is revealed. (1 Peter 1:6-7 NIV)

In the next season of my life, I suffered extreme grief. I didn't know it at the time, but depression had crept in and greatly affected my days in high school. In the next chapter, I explain how grief, trials, and attempted suicide turned to praise, glory, and honor.

# Chapter 6: Out Of Depression Into A Healing Anointing

In 2003, I left my first high school. I received sponsorship for a better, all-girls Catholic high school. But I really hated everything at that high school. Even though God had used me, I needed healing myself. I had become sicker and was depressed. And switching schools made the whole thing worse.

But my mother forced me to go to this school because it was a chance to get sponsorship and better education. It meant going to boarding school, which I really didn't like. I got sick often, and they would call my family to pick me up. I had lost a lot of weight; I was not in good shape.

Mommy used to take me to different pastors, conferences, and healing meetings. She would take me, and she would pray for me too. Still, it seemed like nothing was happening—nothing was changing. I didn't understand that one of the things I was dealing with was called depression. I had been extremely sick and was really depressed, so they brought me home.

I used to have a lot of hate and resentment in my heart towards myself and everyone else. One day I stood up in class and said," I hate you all." After they brought me home from the hospital, I said, "I've had enough. I'm going to put an end to this." I had made it my mission to end my life. I had a plan to overdose on a full bottle of medication. I left the house and went to a building next to an office my mom was sharing with others so I could die alone without anyone interfering. I took the overdose.

When the medicine started kicking in, I was in a little office. People had not yet started work for the day. I knelt and just collapsed on the ground. The next thing I remember is someone waking me up and calling my name. One of my mom's colleagues had found me and woke me up. "Is everything okay? I found you on the ground passed out. You're not okay. You were passed out on the floor. Come, I'll bring your home." I was nauseous. He kept saying, "Something is wrong." He carried me home to my mother.

Mommy was terrified. She got me into bed. I kept saying, "Yeah, I'm fine." But I wasn't okay; I was dying. My big sister, Grace, was so terrified. "Leanny, what's going on. Talk to me," she said. I whispered, "I took an overdose." "Oh my God, are you crazy? Why would you do that? Mommy come, she took an overdose, do something!" she yelled.

So my mommy did first aid. She got milk and mixed it with cooking oil, and flushed it down my throat. They held me and forced me to drink this awful mixture, and I vomited.

No ambulance or hospital would pump my stomach because we couldn't afford it. They had to come up with a solution. So I ended up vomiting a lot and passed out. I slept for a long time.

My mom would come to check to see if I was still breathing. I woke up and opened my eyes; I wondered if I was dead. My mother was sitting next to me. She was extremely upset. "How dare you! How would you do such a thing?" she fumed. I didn't speak a single word. Tears were rolling down my eyes. "Why would you try something like that?" she questioned. She didn't want to vocalize suicide. I just cried. I was just so sad; I just wanted to die to stop all the pain—it was as simple as that.

I had been battling heaviness and sickness for seven years. I was so tired of needles and hospitals. Everything was too much; I wanted it to end because I felt like I was a burden. But that wasn't the truth. Sometimes, the enemy makes you think that everyone is against you, especially when you are depressed and isolated. "If you die, no one will miss you," he whispers. "Look, they all have their appointments and things to do." My mom had spent a lot of money, and it wasn't getting better. "It's not helping anyone. It will be better if you die," the devil said. But by God's grace, even though I tried to act on what the devil whispered, someone found me in that office and took me to my mother.

*Deuteronomy 31:6-8, "I will never leave you nor forsake you..."*

In 2004, I was extremely sick—again. The next day they were going to transfer me to the hospital. I thought, "I have to take my life and make sure it really works this time." I went to the school dispensary and got all the medicine that was there. It was my second time attempting suicide.

I was sitting down and had the medicine with me. But before I had a chance to really swallow it, I heard, "Leanny, Leanny, has anyone seen Leanny? Leanny has disappeared. I can't find her in the school clinic." I was sobbing, crying, and I couldn't see a way out. My friend came and found me with all the medicine in my hand.

"Leanny, I've been looking for you. I had a feeling something was wrong. What do you have in your hand?" I started crying and said, "I'm tired." She slapped all the medicines out of my hand. "Leanny, don't do this. We love you. You're my best friend. I love you." I knew in my heart that that week, I was going to do everything in my power to end my life. I can't explain it, but I just had this thing telling me to kill myself and make everything better.

The next morning my brother came to pick me up and take me to the hospital. They did a full-body scan, checking everything, my blood, urine, and stomach. I had a lot of stomach pain. When I left school, they thought I was going to die. It was on a Monday. The doctor said to my mom, "She has bacteria in her stomach which are eating her intestines. They are eating the flesh inside of her. There are holes in her intestines, and we don't have a solution. Take her home and come back with her in three days. Make it comfortable for her. We'll run other tests."

They expected that I would die in three days; that's why they told my mom to make me comfortable. I was planning to take myself out during those days anyway. On Wednesday, I had a little misunderstanding at home with my brother. I had been planning since morning to have a chance to say goodbye to my younger brother because if my oldest brother found out my plans to kill myself, he would have interrupted me, and I didn't want that. In response to the misunderstanding, I said to my brother, "Leave me alone. I didn't do what you say I did," and walked away. Then, I called my younger brother and said, "Come, I want to say something to you." I gave him a hug and told him how much I loved him and would miss him. I told him, "I'm going to kill myself. It's time for me to go, and I will miss you, but this is the only way out for me." But he was too young to understand what I meant. We hugged each other for about a minute.

I went to my mother's bedroom and got out my medicine. I got a very sharp knife from the kitchen and a bedsheet. I was going to take the painkillers—this time, I wanted to do it very well. The last time was too painful and took too long. I had all these ideas. If the painkillers are taking too long, I'm going to stab myself or strangle myself. I put everything on the bed.

Before I took the medicine in my hand, I heard my brothers and cousin calling my name. They were trying to find me. I didn't want to be interrupted, so I used my brother's mosquito net to hide. I hadn't got a chance to lock the door. When they went away, I passed out. It was like someone gave me a knock on the head. I can't say I fell asleep. Something happened; I just passed out.

The next thing I knew, I was in a different place. It was so beautiful. Everyone was dressed in white. It was like the most giant football field you've ever seen. There was a choir worshipping; they were singing. I've never heard a choir sing so beautifully like that ever before. They were singing "Hallelujah Chorus" by G.F. Handel and Reginald McAll. It was beautiful—the instruments and harmonies were amazing. They were all in white; they were just shining. I could see that I was the only person in my normal clothes, which were not white.

The choirmaster signaled to me; wait over there, I'm coming. I was still looking in awe of the place. Then he said, "Come with me." He was wearing a very white suit and speaking my native Ugandan language even though he looked light-skinned. It felt like he knew everything about me—my whole life. He could speak to my heart without saying a word out loud.

He took my hand, and we instantly appeared in my mother's house; we were back home. My mother was sitting on her sofa. There was a very muscular man standing beside her, and I knew it was her guardian angel. This was not the choirmaster I met in heaven. Then the choirmaster says three times, "I am here to heal your daughter." I started to jump up and down and shouted, "Yes, yes, yes, I'm healed."

"God sent me to heal your daughter, and the reason she's been sick is because of this demon." He pointed to the corner. Out of nowhere, this half-naked woman jumped out. She stood in front of me, abusing me with her body language, trying to intimidate me. I said, "You demon in the name of Jesus, never come back into my life." Just like that, she disappeared.

The choirmaster kept talking and said, "From today on, you will never be sick again. I have taken it all today." I realized this person had been Jesus the whole time; he introduced himself to me. It was like he knew everything about me. He could speak to my heart. He said, "From now on, you will never suffer again. I have taken it all today, but remember to serve me. Tell them about me, serve me." I woke up; I stood up. The whole bed was wet from my sweat as if I had been in a war.

I checked myself to see if I was totally free. I did not have a single pain. I could stand up, sit up, dance; everything was gone. I could still feel his presence in the room. He walked with me to the bed where I had everything to kill myself, and I could audibly hear him.

He called me by my nickname, the name my parents gave me, and I could feel him. "Why were you going to kill yourself?" He repeated the same question. "Why were you going to kill yourself?" Every time he spoke, my heart was filled with conviction, and I knew that I wouldn't have made it to heaven if I had killed myself. I cried and said, "Lord, I'm so sorry. Please forgive me. May you be just when you judge." "Don't you know that God loves you? Why were you going to kill yourself?" I couldn't come up with an answer. I felt I had a right to take my life, but I was wrong. After I apologized and repented, peace came over me.

I told my siblings what had happened, and they were excited for me. When my mom came home, I told her too. At first, she didn't believe me. She thought I was losing my mind because of the pain. She had prayed that I would die so the pain would go away.

We went back to the hospital, and they ran new tests for my whole body again (like before). The doctor read the results, looked at me, and shook her head. She asked me to step out of the room to talk to my mom. Afterward, as the doctor talked to my mother, she said, "I'm sorry, I know you have spent a lot of money. Maybe it's all in her head? But I can't explain what made her healthy again because we have two results. The old one says she's severely sick, and the new one says everything is fine and normal. Maybe she didn't like the school, maybe that's why she was getting sick. I have a psychiatric doctor that maybe can help. This is a good friend of mine. She can talk to you. Let me try to talk to your daughter," she said to my mom. The doctor called me in and asked, "How are you feeling?" "I am very fine," I said. She looked at me, confused. I asked her, "Doctor, do you believe in God? Do you believe in miracles?" She replied, "I go to church once a year at Christmas." "Jesus healed me, and I am fine. And I do believe in God and in miracles," I said to her. After that, she proceeded to write down the contact of her friend, the psychiatric doctor.

My mom was furious. As we left the hospital, she said, "I am so upset with you right now. All this time, you were not sick; you were pretending to be sick. I'm so upset with you right now. Even if you are sick tomorrow, I will not bring you to the hospital," she said. I looked at mommy and said, "I told you Jesus healed me, but you don't believe me." She looked at me, got quiet, and said, "Let's go for lunch." That day we had a girls' day out; we had lunch in the city center. I had a clean bill of health. I asked mommy how I could have explained the holes and the bacteria. I was not pretending; this could only be God. No one can explain. It's supernatural; it's God, I told her.

A week later, I went back to boarding school. The first person who saw me screamed and ran off. When the headteacher saw me, she panicked. They were screaming and running off in terror like they saw a ghost. Someone came and pinched my face. "They told us you died. We even held a vigil for you," they said.

There was a mix-up; there was another student who was fighting bone cancer. When she passed away, they announced that I died. This girl died in the time that God met me and took me to heaven. I would have been dead if God had not intervened. I told them my story. I was supposed to be dead that week, but Jesus healed me and changed my story. Jesus came to the ghetto where I was going to end my life. All the times I was going to kill myself, he came right to the dirty places I was in and rescued me. He put everything down and rescued me. I started sharing my testimony with my classmates, which was the beginning of a turning point and revival in my entire high school.

> Deuteronomy 31:8, " *It is the Lord who goes before you. He will be with you; he will not fail you or forsake you. Do not fear or be dismayed.*"

I thought I would share, and that would be it. But one Saturday morning, I was taking a shower (the school had outside bathrooms). I didn't realize that I had been left alone and was washing my underwear. I heard a person speak audibly, "I want you to pray for them. They are sick; they have pain in their stomach." I looked around and said, who is there? The voice spoke again—repeating the same thing. I wonder, is it me? Am I going to be sick? I cancel it in the name of Jesus, I thought. The voice repeated the same thing, and I said, "I am very shy. They won't listen to me because I don't even have the power to heal people." The voice replied, "If I gave you the power to heal the sick and make the lame walk, what more power do you need?" I said, "I don't know what to say." The voice said, "I will give you what to say." I got so scared, I just poured the water out and ran away.

I got back to the dormitory but was still processing what happened. When I arrived, someone was walking door to door, asking, "Does anyone want to preach tomorrow?" I can still remember the voice saying, I want you to pray for them. She came to me and said, "Sister, do you want to preach tomorrow?" I said, "No." I felt my heart beating out of my chest. She turned and started to walk away; I started sweating and feeling like my heart might explode if I didn't speak up and stop her. So I said, "Wait. Yes, sister. Yes, I will preach tomorrow," I said. She started rejoicing. "Okay, give me your name."

But another twist came. My teacher announced that we had an emergency exam the same day I was supposed to preach. I finished up early, ready to leave, but the teacher says, "No one is leaving this room until everyone is finished." I kept looking at the clock, and I knew I would be late to preach. But I had no other option. No matter what, I had to go preach. I had made God a promise, and I had to keep it. As I finally came into the service, they were saying the closing prayer; they were finished. "Sorry, sister, we waited for you, but you were late," the sister said.

"Wait, can I say something. Is there someone here who has pain in their stomach?" I asked. And again, I asked and waited. Nobody turned; they kept walking out of the room. "See God, I did my part," I said to him. I turned to leave the pulpit, and someone tapped my shoulder and said, "Me."

Immediately, I prayed, "In the name of Jesus, I pray for healing. Stomach pain, be gone in the name of Jesus." Another person came and said, "Me too." It felt as if when I laid my hands on the second person, electricity hit me in the middle of my head. I was shocked. I had never experienced anything like that before; I knew God was in the room. I realized the Holy Spirit was touching people. The girl I prayed for jumped and fell down, and demons started manifesting out of her. She was rolling, and by that time, people started coming. Anybody I touched was just falling. They were carrying people after people. We prayed until midnight; the headteacher encouraged me to keep praying for people, saying I had to finish what I started. There was a girl born with crossed eyes. They got uncrossed that night.

There were so many people. The Holy Spirit told me to pray for others I knew God was using. I didn't know about impartation; I was following the Holy Spirit. When I laid hands on them and prayed for them that the Lord would use them the way he was using me, they also prayed for people. We were there for hours. But thankfully, the generator didn't work the next morning, so we could sleep in and rest.

More miracles happened in that school! There was a girl with a deformed foot who couldn't walk straight. One day God told me to pray for her. So I waited for her to come back from the bathroom. "Would you like Jesus to make your foot better?" I asked. I knelt down and started to pray for her as my friends watched. When they saw me pray for her, they all gathered around and held hands so I could have privacy to pray for her. When I prayed for her, I got so hot. I started shaking, and I said, "Walk." She was still limping a bit, so I said, "Come back. Can I take off your shoes?" I took her foot in my hands. My hands were so hot. I prayed for her, and I could feel the bones moving and hear them cracking. The school had gathered, and I became overwhelmed. I started crying, and she started crying. Everyone was in an uproar because God healed her, and she walked straight!

The teachers came and had to hide us because everyone wanted to see us. They interrogated her and me separately. They asked me," How do you do that? How did you make her walk? We're going to call your parents." I kept telling them, "It was not me. It was Jesus, I just prayed, and she walked." The revival started.

When I came to that high school, it was known for having immoral happenings and sexual perversion. The Lord started cleaning out the school. They used to have a disco; it was canceled. Instead, they let us use the hall for Bible studies, services, and conferences.

Still, some teachers didn't approve. Two teachers hated me. One of them tried to get me expelled from school. They took me and my friends who believed in Jesus to a meeting, and all the students in the meeting said they believed in God. They started interrogating and threatening that if we denied Jesus, they would let us go back to class, but they would expel us if not. Please remember, this was a Catholic school.

Only one friend broke; the rest of them stood firm. They labeled me as the ringleader and took me to the school leader. "So you are Leanny?" he said. "I've heard so many things about you; it's a pleasure to finally meet you. So tell me, how did you make a girl walk?" I started laughing and explained what happened. "Wow, this is really inspiring. This is not even bad because they wanted me to expel you from school, but I don't see a reason to expel you. It doesn't make sense. The way they described you, I thought you were this bad, mean person. Would you like lunch?" he said. "No, I'm fasting," I replied. "Could you pray for me? My daughter is sick. Could you just pray for my family and bless us?" he replied. So when I walked out of the meeting, everyone was like, oh no, she's gone. But they failed to get me expelled from school. I found favor, and the school leader instead asked for prayer.

> Psalm 32:7-8, "*You are my hiding place; you will protect me from trouble and surround me with songs of deliverance.*"

God is faithful; if he has told you to do something, trust that he will be true to his promise and take care of you. Don't be afraid to express your faith. God promised to never leave you or forsake you at any time. He is with you; trust Him. He turned my grief, trials, and depression during those high school days to praise, honor, and glory. In the next season, I would graduate from high school and start working. But I would receive more than wages.

# Section 3: Graduating To The Next Phase

# Chapter 7: More Than Wages

*God can do anything, you know—far more than you could ever imagine or guess or request in your wildest dreams! (Ephesians 3:20 The Message Bible)*

In 2004, I graduated from that Catholic high school. My mom got me into a program that helped with school fees, but the charity's help didn't pay for everything. My older brother, Martin, who by that time lived in England, helped pay the difference. So I was able to graduate; it was an expensive school. I've always been grateful for that.

In Uganda, after you graduate, you have a full year off (vacation); you don't go directly to school or university. I got a job working in an internet café, helping and copying files. My mom helped me pay for a course to learn Microsoft Word. So I started teaching people how to do things on the computer like typing emails, etc. I basically was working for two things: experience and food.

In Africa, you often don't get paid at the end of the day. Employers come with excuses. I was only earning $1 and using that money for transport and food. So I was literary working for nothing, but I gained experience. My focus was on acquiring skills. My mom always said, "God had better plans for us and to look ahead. There is always something better; you don't settle for less. Get up and keep moving. Keep trusting God." So I had that in the back of my mind.

A friend of mine (a family friend) came, and I could help him with typing. He was in church with my mom. He came and told me there was a job opening. A church had opened an Internet café, and if I wanted, I could apply.

I didn't have perfect qualifications, so I printed out all my courses, papers, certificates and talked to God. I remember I had my papers in a file. I told my mom I was going to a job interview, but I didn't tell her where. I didn't want my mom's knowing the pastor to interfere. I didn't want her to say, "This is my child. Can you help her?" I prayed and said, "If this job is for me, then you're gonna give it to me."

I walked into the waiting area for the interview, and there were many people with all these qualifications. I only had God in my corner. After the interview, they told me, "You have passed the interview. For me, I would give you the job immediately, but I have to confirm with my co-workers."

I proceeded for a second interview. In the middle of the second interview, a white guy walked in. I didn't think much of him. He came in and went back out. After the interview, they said, "You have the job." I wanted to scream, but I didn't want to lose my composure. "This is how much we'll be paying you, 150,000 shillings a month ($50 a month). Fifty thousand at the beginning of the month and 100,000 at the end of the month." It was an upgrade; I could help my mom at home. It was good; we had a fixed income now. My mom was really, really happy.

During that time, I was also in ministry. I went to work part-time and did ministry when I was free. One day I came from a service at a local church in the slums, and miracles had really happened; it was awesome. There was a young boy born deaf in one ear. He regained his hearing. Sometimes you just want to share these things with someone. I came to work, and I wanted to share these things with someone.

My boss came in and said, "You look happy." I asked him if he had ever experienced God doing something in his life and just wanted to shout it out and let everyone know how good God is. "I don't know, I've never experienced something like that. Okay, tell me what happened; what did God do?" he said. I told him, and he looked at me and said, "Wow, that's really, really great."

I told him my testimony about how God had healed me and set me free from suicide. He said, "Next Saturday I'm invited to speak. How about you come with me and take my place to speak because I believe everyone will really benefit from your testimony." "But they invited you? Will it be okay?" I asked. I told him I wouldn't come alone; I would bring my older brother with me. "Don't worry, I'm not coming alone either. I will also bring a friend of mine," he said.

I learned that my boss came to Uganda to seek the Lord. He wanted to travel to Canada, but he ended up coming to

Uganda. Since his church was working with a local Ugandan church, they asked him if he would like to use his time in Uganda to help and supervise their work in Uganda. So I had planned to go to Canada after graduating but ended up staying in Uganda. And my boss, who wanted to go to Canada, ended up in Uganda.

So I brought my brother to the speaking engagement; my boss brought his friend. There were about 300 people at the conference. It was in a school. They were asking him, "Do you know who your friend is? Leanny is a woman of God," and they started sharing testimonies with him about what had happened to them.

After I ministered, people gave their lives to the Lord, and it rained very heavily. My boss was used to driving private cars, but we had to take a taxi overloaded with people. Someone in the taxi was holding a live chicken. They put my boss in the middle of four people. I was sitting behind, and my brother was sitting in front. Nobody warned my boss not to sit in the middle. Another man was holding a basket, and one had a baby goat. The chicken was making noise and disturbing everyone.

So my boss switched places and came to where I was sitting. My brother looked behind. I was cold and shivering. My boss said, "Put your hands in my hands; I will keep you warm." I didn't think much about it and said, "Sure." And I just put my hands in his hands. He started rubbing my hands. The taxi continued going with a live chicken and goat inside.

"What are we doing?" my boss said, "I don't know. Holding hands." I replied. I didn't know that in his culture, it meant something else. So I didn't think much of it when he asked what we were doing. Afterward, he told me, "No, no, no, no, you go home. I will work your shift. You need to rest." I got home and told mommy the testimonies. We knelt down, gave thanks, and prayed for all the things God had done—the number of miracles that night was overwhelming.

And the next day at work, another small miracle would take place.

> ... we know God is working behind the scenes. (Job 34:20, MSG)

# Chapter 8: Would You Like Ice Cream?

The next day I went to work, and my boss was already there waiting for me. He asked, "Would you like ice cream?" I found it a little strange because he was very reserved, especially when it came to women co-workers. I always felt that he was sad. I remember one time as co-workers we were talking, and I thought, he's always alone. He never goes out or dates anyone—what's wrong with him. I didn't say it out loud, but I thought it. So when he asked me for ice cream, I thought, sure. He came with cones, and the ice cream was melting down his arm.

That evening he offered to give me a lift home. He usually dropped off the male co-workers. "I don't want you to travel alone in the night. I will drive you home," he said. So he drove me home. I started noticing things. If I talked to a male client, he would come around inspecting things. They would comment that my boss would angrily look at them. I didn't know much about men. My brother said, "You know what, Leanny, I think he has feelings for you. I think he likes you."

African men would approach you and say what they want. But my boss was from a different culture. One evening, he said, "I want to talk to you." I had already started suspecting because of the extra care he was giving, opening doors, etc. So he said, "What do you think about us?" He told me he had feelings for me and that when he came to Uganda, he didn't come to find a wife; he came to seek God. So we talked and shared. We both had these butterflies. "Lydia, I prayed that God gives me a wife who loves him with all her heart," he shared.

I think he fell in love with me because of my calling. If a man first falls in love with your calling as a minister, that is particularly good because he won't have problems with you ministering. I grew up seeing my uncle beating his wife and abusing her. I watched movies of white men being caring and romantic. I wanted someone who would love me and support me in ministry.

My mom always said, talk to God about your prayer request, about what you want. I grew up with a faith that if you ask God for something, he will answer. Trust and wait upon the Lord.

So we started dating. I used to go home by seven o'clock. But we were talking one night, and he brought me home late, around midnight. We just lost track of time talking and sharing about life and everything. I had butterflies in my stomach; I had never felt like that before. When I got home, I shared all this with my sister, and she said, "You're in love; that's why you feel butterflies in your stomach. Just drink warm water to calm your stomach." My mother was furious. She was yelling, "Do you know what time it is?"

I talked to my mother because I didn't know how to explain to her that I was dating a white boy. She was quiet when I told her. I thought, "Oh my God, she's going to kill me." She said, "You think I'm stupid? I already know what's going on." There was this open silence. She said God had already told her about him and what was going on. She told me to pray about it and ask God if he was the right person.

Old-school Ugandans, especially older people, believe that white men are not well-cultured or respectful. In my tribe, parents are not supposed to shake hands with the person you are dating. For example, when their son is dating a woman, the father is not supposed to have physical contact with the woman. When their daughter is dating a man, the mother is not supposed to have physical contact with the man. However, when my boyfriend met my mother, he tried to shake hands with her. He thought, why is your mother hiding? She was keeping her distance, sitting in the next room watching. I had to explain that the parents of the person you are dating are not supposed to have physical contact to shake hands, etc. That's why my mother always had to sit in another room whenever my boyfriend came around. He was still shocked.

She warmed up to him eventually and realized it was cultural differences. So she accepted shaking hands with him but not in public. And he got used to my family. Sometimes people would yell across the street, "Take all his money and leave him dry." Some would yell things like, "These white men come and take all our beautiful women." We were walking with my elder brother, and a guy yelled a racist slur at my boss, who was now my boyfriend. He was saying racist things about white people and how much he hated whites. My elder brother grabbed the guy and almost started fighting him. My immediate family and I didn't see my boyfriend as white anymore. He was just part of our family. So it infuriated my brother.

Remember, my boss (and now my new boyfriend) was working for his Swiss church in Uganda. Together with a local Ugandan church, the Swiss church had asked him to help manage the work at the Internet café since he was in Uganda. So he told them that we were dating. They said they were okay with it; it was fine. They welcomed me at first. So the time came for my boyfriend to return to Switzerland. He stayed in Uganda for nine months. We had started dating in March, but he had to go back. We prayed and asked the Lord to give him a job.

He used to struggle with depression. He told my mom and me that he had these phases. We would fast and pray with him, and God delivered him. We grew together more in the spirit and became remarkably close. He returned and got a job the next month, and we continued dating long-distance.

*A friend loves at all times, and a brother is born for adversity. (Proverbs 17:17 ESV)*

The story of our relationship took a new turn after he went back to Switzerland.

# Chapter 9: A Switzerland Breakup?

*There is neither Jew nor Gentile, neither slave nor free, nor is there male and female, for you are all one in Christ Jesus. (Galatians 3:28 NIV)*

After returning to Switzerland, my boyfriend wanted me to travel there to meet his family. My mom and family were okay with it. So I came to Switzerland in 2006 for three months as a tourist. It was at the end of 2006. It had been about a eight months since we started dating. He took off one month from work to show me around and meet his family.

The first month was so great, but the next month he had to ask a family he knew from his church if I could stay with them to respect our Christian standard of holiness. It was imperative that we not stay together in the same apartment. He was living with his parents, and I lived with a family from his church. They couldn't speak English, and I couldn't speak German at the time. So there was often miscommunication. For example, I would be asking for a towel, and they would bring me soap. Cross-cultural communication and relationships have their challenges.

The pastors and leaders of his church had gotten to know me in Uganda. But when I reached Switzerland, they changed; they were totally against our relationship. They started fighting the relationship. They used to call us from time to time—the leaders, the pastors' wife—and ask about how the relationship was. They could all speak English but didn't want to speak English around me. They would speak Swiss German, and I would hear my name every now and again in the conversation. So clearly, I knew they were talking about me. It always made me sad. So the pastors scrutinized every move I made. I felt like I was interrogated.

Everything I did was under scrutiny. They were treating me like it was the best thing to come to Europe; you're coming from Africa, so you must appreciate that you are coming to Europe. They wanted me to speak German—no English. But you can't just expect a person to learn your language from day one.

After one month into my visit, he went back to work. I had to live with a family that didn't speak good English. The pastor's wife would use the lady of this house to spy on me. Whenever they called us into a meeting and asked about the relationship, they would say I didn't want to really live in Europe or learn the language. They pressured our relationship and made us both feel like what we were doing—being in an interracial relationship—was a crime.

The pastor had a lot of control over the people in the church, especially the church leaders. By then, my boyfriend had been in that church more than seven years and trusted what they had to say. So the pastor used that to manipulate him. He knew his opinion mattered to my boyfriend because he was his pastor. He told the church leaders what we were doing was wrong and was not of

God because black and white didn't belong together. He used to say, "Cross-cultural marriages don't work out." At first, we didn't realize he was saying these things. We didn't realize he was telling people to tell us these things. He made us think that everyone else was against us.

The husband and wife I stayed with while visiting were elders in the church. The pastors would call them and tell them to discourage what we were doing. So when my boyfriend would come over for dinner, they would ask all kinds of questions. He asked the elder what he thought about our relationship. The elder said, "I don't believe it's from God. You guys should break up." We didn't have any personal issues, but the people in his church were very much against the relationship. But both our families were incredibly supportive and didn't understand why the people in his church were behaving as if it was a crime. His parents only asked if he loved me and was happy. But his church's reaction was taking a toll on him—he was torn between his biological family and his church family. He was so excited and would take me to meet different people in his church. Still, they were all negative and kept saying interracial marriages wouldn't work.

I didn't understand it because I grew up differently. My family embraced everyone. It didn't really occur to me that I was black until I went to visit. The church elders I was staying with told me I couldn't stay with them anymore. My boyfriend was sad and shocked. He called his parents, and they said I could stay with them. I moved to his parents' home.

Now, I was away from the church members. They would call him a lot. Once we went out on a date, and they pressured him to choose between the church and me. They gave him an ultimatum. They told him he was welcome, but I was not welcome. I was fed up, and when we arrived home to his parents' house, I asked him to call his pastor so we could talk. I called his pastor, and the wife answered and said he was away. So I asked her what their problem was because it says we all belong to one family in the Bible.

She got furious and started yelling at me, saying that I was manipulative. "You Africans use witchcraft; you have bewitched him, and we don't want you here. You're not welcome here. Go back to your country. We love him, and we're trying to protect him from you. So leave him alone, and you're not welcome here," she said. I replied, "First of all, I'm not a witch. I've never used witchcraft. I gave my life to Jesus at five years old." I told her what you guys are doing is called racism, and it's wrong. She started yelling, saying, "How dare you call me a racist. I don't want to talk to you anymore. I want to talk to him." Look, we love African people, she told him. We do business in Africa. How can she say I'm a racist?

I told her that doing business in Africa doesn't mean you love the people. And if she did, she would be treating me differently. She said, "That's it. You're forbidden to come to church, come near any church property, or have contact with anyone in the church. But he is welcome." At that point, I felt she had done me a favor because every time I would go, it was like walking into hell. I would go to the church, and no one would want to sit next to me or talk to me. I didn't want to go where I was not wanted. There were only two African people in the church. I was the only African adult, and there was a young boy who was adopted from Ethiopia.

I found out that in the past, if anyone dated someone who was not a member of the church, the couple broke up or they ended up not coming back. So my standing up to them really provoked them and angered them. My boyfriend had to decide.

They pressured him. Each time they called, they would ask," Did you send that African back?" They all knew my name but would refer to me as "That African." He would tell them no and that he loved me. And they would tell him that didn't matter; they were trying to save him. He ended up breaking up with me.

So we broke up. He contacted the airline, and I prepared to go home. It was very tense because we were under the same roof. I was in the guest room at his parent's house. His parents were torn because they saw the pain we were both going through. He was torn, and I was miles away from home. We were both incredibly sad and brokenhearted. We broke up not because we had any problems between us but because of people's opinions in the church. When I would see them in the store, even when I would say hi, they would pretend they never knew me. The church leadership commanded them to do so because they had a rule in the church that no one should have contact with you if you leave the church. The pastor even had a tendency of threatening to sue people and would call people's employers to try to get them fired.

It was now the end of the year, and I spent New Year's Eve alone. They invited him to a New Year's gathering and wanted to reassure him that it was the best decision he had made. I was alone in his parent's house. His mom and dad had gone to celebrate with family members. I prayed and declared that all this madness was gone with the old year. It was a new year, and I believed in God for a change. My now "ex"-boyfriend later came home and apologized, explaining that he was sorry but had to help at church. I told him he didn't have to apologize; we were no longer together, etc. So my return date was quickly approaching.

Instead of being angry with the church people, I started repenting on their behalf and asking God to forgive them. I also called my mom, and we joined together to pray for them. I didn't pray that my ex-boyfriend and I would get back together but that God would save the people in that church.

Three weeks before I traveled back home, I went into fasting and prayer. I fasted and prayed for three days, the way Esther prayed. I wanted to meet his pastor, not to confront him but to make peace before I left; I was resolute. I knew my ex-boyfriend and I were not together. I didn't want to leave with any regrets about not making peace. I told God I wanted to meet the pastor, but I want you to go with me. I want to have peace with them.

I called the pastor, and again his wife answered the phone. She thought it was my boyfriend. She was happy, "Hi!" she joyfully said. She was shocked when she found out it was me. Our last conversation didn't end well. "Oh Lydia, how are you, and how is your family?" she asked. "Everyone is fine. I just want to schedule a meeting with you guys." I replied. "Really?" she said, dumbfounded. "I just want to talk because I'm soon returning home, and I would like to see you guys before that," I said. I gave her the date that would have been the third day of my fasting.

My ex-boyfriend's mom was extremely nervous about it. But she helped me get ready on the third day. The first day, I had a dream and saw two angels that came. One took off his coat and dropped it on my feet. I picked it up. They started talking, "God knows you're here and why you are here. God loves you and knows why you are here, and he is here. God is here. That's why he named you Daniel. You're seeing a new journey." I woke up. I knew that I wasn't in the wrong place after that. I wrote down the dream so I wouldn't forget it.

On the third day, I met the pastor's wife. She was extra nice and asked if I wanted to eat, but I just wanted to go to her office. So we went to the office, and she asked how I was and how I was doing. I said, "First of all, I'm here in peace. I'm not here to fight or argue or anything like that. The Bible says we should make peace with all men, and all will be well with us. I'm going home soon, and I would like to talk about what happened between us." She was like yeah, it's okay. I continued, "First of all, I want to apologize if I said anything out of frustration, but I want you to know I don't have any hatred in my heart." She started crying. I said, "You don't have to cry or feel sorry for me." She said, "No, I feel so bad about what we did to you. On behalf of the church leadership, please forgive us." I said, "It's okay. I forgave you already before I came here. I pray to God that he forgives you too." She asked, "So how is your relationship?" And I answered, "There's no more relationship."

"I can't let that happen," she responded.
"You don't have to do anything; we decided it's the best thing for both of us," I said.
"No, I can't let that happen." she insisted.

Then, she invited my ex-boyfriend to come in. They talked, and she told him, if you let Lydia go back to Uganda with you not dating, you might lose her forever. You have our full support to date, marry, or whatever. So she kind of gave us a blessing. He said he had to talk to me about it. So we went home. His parents were anxiously awaiting to hear what happened when I went to talk to the pastor's wife.

When we got back, I asked for dinner. So we sat down, I ate, and they were all waiting. I told them what happened. And my ex-boyfriend says, "You know we are back together. We are dating." And I said, "We are?" We made a toast and celebrated.

> *Go, gather together all the Jews that are present in Shushan, and fast ye for me, and neither eat nor drink three days, night or day: I also and my maidens will fast likewise; and so will I go in unto*

> the king, which is not according to the law: and if I perish, I perish.17 So Mordecai went his way, and did according to all that Esther had commanded him. 1 Now it came to pass on the third day, that Esther put on her royal apparel, and stood in the inner court of the king's house, over against the king's house: and the king sat upon his royal throne in the royal house, over against the gate of the house. 2 And it was so, when the king saw Esther the queen standing in the court, that she obtained favour in his sight: and the king held out to Esther the golden sceptre that was in his hand. So Esther drew near, and touched the top of the sceptre.
> (Esther 4:16-5:2 KJV)

That day there was a turnaround. After three days of fasting and prayer, God melted the pastor's wife's heart, and I could return to Uganda in peace. The blessing was released for the next phase of our relationship.

# Chapter 10: Marriage: Yays And Nays

"Do you think you will be happy here, spending life with me in a foreign land? Do you like it here? Do you like Switzerland?" my boyfriend asked.

"Yes," I replied.
He grabbed my hand and exuded, "Let's go tell them!"
"Tell them what?" I asked, perplexed.
"That we are getting married. Come on. Let's go!"

That was two days before I was to return to Uganda from my three months in Switzerland. We left his room and went to his parents' room.

"Mom, paps, we are getting married," he said.
"What took you so long to make up your mind? You did the right thing." his father replied.

We celebrated; there was a toast! So I returned to Uganda engaged. A month before that, I was separated, broken up in a foreign land. And now I was getting married. Our families were happy.

After I got back to Uganda, we started to plan two weddings. We had a traditional wedding in Uganda (That's the first wedding you have in Uganda before the legal wedding, with a dowry, gifts, etc.) We got married in May, so by the end of April, everything was underway. My mother was so proud and very happy. A week before my fiancé traveled to Uganda, he told me, "Honey, I feel sick. My lymph nodes are swollen, and I don't feel good." I said, "Before you travel, have the doctors check you out." He said he would go but felt sick and no appetite.

The next day, he went to the doctor and explained what was happening. The doctor told him his lymph nodes were really swollen, and he would like to run some tests. He sent him to a specialist, an oncologist. They discovered he had a tumor—it was cancerous. They gave him the results and told him they didn't yet know what kind of cancer it was and whether it's treatable. This was two weeks before our wedding.

After leaving the doctor's office, he called while my sister and I were out shopping for the wedding. He said, "Honey, I got the results. I have cancer." I went silent. It was just a shock. He started to cry; I cried too. I put the phone on speaker. My sister asked what's going on and if he was okay. He told her he had cancer. Immediately, she started crying.

He wanted to talk to me alone, so I took the phone off speaker mode. He told me he loved me and didn't want to do this to me because I was young. He didn't know if he would live and didn't want to make me a widow. He wanted me to know I was free to make whatever decision I wanted, and he wouldn't force me to stay with him if I wanted to rethink the whole thing. He made it clear that he would hold no grudges against me. He didn't know what would happen with his life now and didn't want to put me in a bad position. He told me if I wanted to walk away, I was free, and he wouldn't hold it against me.

I thought about it, and I wasn't going anywhere. I wasn't going to love my fiancé only in good times. So I told him I wasn't going anywhere. I trusted God that he would not give me an engagement and not let there be a victory. God's hand had been with us all the way. I knew he would come through somehow. I told him we would continue with the wedding, and we're going to fight this together with God and go through it. We had already been through so much.

The doctor told him it was okay to fly and get married. He could come back and have the surgery to remove the tumor and chemotherapy. Two weeks later, we got married. It was a beautiful wedding. My mom didn't know. Only my sister, brother, husband, and I knew what was going on. I had three dresses. In a traditional wedding, you change several times. He had never seen such a wedding before.

My mother gave him something like a "Prince of Zamunda" festival. My mom wanted it to have a royal style. She had great taste and knew how to throw a good party. She hired a whole band, which picked him up (carried him) like a king with drumming. And for a moment, we forgot about cancer and just enjoyed the "royal treatment" for the day. I felt like a princess. My sister was my maid of honor; it was beautiful. There were 300 people! But according to my husband, it was extremely hot because he had to wear all the traditional clothes he wasn't used to. My family told him, "If you want to marry one of us, you must dress like one of us this day."

A week later, he returned to Switzerland and immediately had the operation. I was waiting for my visa in Uganda, which made it even harder because I couldn't be with him for the operation. His parents were there. I had told my mom what was happening. She protested why I didn't tell her sooner, but I told her I wanted her to enjoy the wedding.

He started chemotherapy. I had never seen anyone go through chemotherapy. He lost a lot of weight; all his hair—even his eyebrows came off. He went to shower one day, and all his hair was in his hands, so his mom shaved his hair. We prayed. I cried with my mother and prayed. I had just turned twenty years old, and he was thirty years old. I prayed and declared, there's no way you would give me a husband and let him die. I got my visa and came as quickly as I could. On top of all that was going on, we had another wedding coming up in Switzerland. We were doing another one there so his family could attend. He had gotten an apartment, but he was not in good shape.

The chemo made him tired all the time. He was vomiting and having to take so much medication. He was sleeping most of the day. All this while trying to plan a second wedding. We had to depend on the church and family to help. The chemo also affected his ear hair (in the eardrum) and made his ears extremely sensitive. Now, by the grace of God, the sensitivity has left, and he has regained his hearing.

We had thought that the church was okay now, but the pastor still had his grudge. His wife had gone ahead and apologized, but he was still holding on and was not going to let us have a happy ending. The pastor called my husband's cell phone and started yelling at him, "Stop stressing people out. Your wife is stressing people asking them to help with your church wedding. By the way, I'm not going to officiate the wedding. It's wrong; it's not from God. Cross-cultural marriages don't work out. After five years, she's going to steal all your money, divorce you, go back to Africa, marry an African, and bring him here." Stephan replied, "These people volunteered. They wanted to help, and besides, the only people Lydia knows here are the people in the church."

Some people helped us with the afterparty food and snacks. But it was so bad because the pastor somehow said to the people that the marriage was wrong and stopped some people from helping us. Only a few didn't listen and continued helping us. When my husband asked so-called friends to be his best man, they had all kinds of excuses. Even the church photographer refused to take pictures. Some of them would say on the side, this is not right, but never openly stood up to say it was wrong.

I told my husband it was too much stress; we should focus on him getting healthy. I also told him the pastor had no right to do what he was doing. He never called to ask how my husband was doing or pray for him but would call to pester him about not getting married. So I told my husband that when he was fine again, we would have a church wedding with people who were happy for us and really loved us. They were not true friends. Friends are supportive. So we ended up postponing the church wedding. I didn't want to have a church wedding with people who are hypocrites. How could we have a wedding full of people who were saying the marriage was not of God. So we decided to postpone the church wedding and have only the civil wedding at that time.

Two days before our civil wedding, we were getting ready to go shopping for my husband for the wedding. We got a call from the pastor saying he would like to see my husband. He told the pastor I was coming with him because we were going shopping for the wedding. He told my husband he didn't want to see me; he just wanted to see him. We drove to the pastor's house amidst heavy rain. My husband went inside to talk to the pastor.

The pastor tells my husband that he called him there because he loved him, was missing him, and wanted to protect him. He told my husband he should not proceed with the wedding. It would be the biggest mistake of his life. My husband was puzzled, wondering what he was talking about. He continued, telling my husband that I would divorce him and steal all his money. And Africans want a good life in Europe. My husband said, "We've already married before God and her family in Africa." The pastor replied, "That doesn't matter. What matters is the civil wedding. That's what's official. That's what matters most." "But pastor, you know what you're saying is really hurting me right now. You know that I love Lydia, and I don't want to divorce her. I'm in love with her, and you just have to accept it," my husband responded. "Okay, you can do it, but you have to make this promise to me. Do not trust her. Don't trust her with your bank account, your pin code. You have to be very careful," the pastor said.

After about two hours, my husband came out, and we went shopping. Two days later, we had our civil wedding.

# Section 4: Becoming One: A New Chapter

# Chapter 11: Give Me Your Heart: Loss And Gain

*Keep thy heart with all diligence; for out of it are the issues of life. – Proverbs 4:23*

We continued to attend my husband's church in Switzerland, but I hated it. The pastor still had a mindset that it was necessary to destroy our marriage. He told church members that they had to get rid of me and save my husband—although from what I don't know.

I had relocated, left everything I knew, and the only home I knew to be with my husband in a foreign country. I felt a lot of pain because the pastor was intent on breaking me. One day, I was washing dishes and holding a glass. I squeezed it until it broke because all his words kept replaying in my mind. "You're not wanted here. You're not welcome here. Go back to Africa." Even worse than his words were his actions. There were times he would hug everyone in the church and skip me or even hug my husband and ignore me.

For some time, it greatly affected me and our marriage. It brought a strain to the beginning of our marriage. It was like our honeymoon phase was stolen. Whenever my husband would go to church without me, it was their chance to talk to him and ask him questions. They would say, "You see. We warned you and tried to protect you from these things." My husband would come home with a different demeanor because they had been feeding him negative ideas. I would ask him, "What's wrong; did I do something?"

It began to reduce me and diminish my strength to live out my calling. I was removed from a support system and family. I was in a foreign land, learning a new language with no friends and church leaders who were against me. It's one thing for a jealous ex-girlfriend or someone in the church who used to like your spouse to come against you. But when the pastor and leadership come against you and influence other church members to do so, it feels especially evil, like the Sanhedrin religious network that came against Jesus. The pain and isolation were too much.

So I closed my heart; I wasn't letting anyone in. The pastor used to send people to befriend me just to get information out of me. They would take whatever I said back to him. He really isolated me. When I sat in church, I couldn't focus. I built emotional walls to protect myself from being hurt. I wasn't going to let anyone close to me. I didn't like to attend church events because if my husband was busy with the technical setup, I would be alone. I remember sitting there one day, feeling so alone. I had a vision and saw Jesus standing there in front of me, and he said, "Lydia, I want you to give me your heart." I started crying, and through the tears, I replied.

> "Lord, I can't. I'm scared because if I open my heart, I'm going to love and feel all this pain," I said.
> "Give me your heart; I want to take the pain. You don't have to be afraid," he replied.

"Okay, but I'm scared."

At that moment, it was like I took out my heart and gave it to Jesus, and he did the same. But his heart was so big! He put his heart into mine. I was looking down to the ground. He said, "I want you to look at me. I'm going to protect you. I love you, and I won't let anything happen to you." "I'm scared," I replied. "I know. But when you focus your eyes on me, anything that would try to hurt you would have to go through me. You just focus your eyes on me, and you know that nothing can come through me to get you. So you just focus on me and let me do everything for you," he said. It was as if everything just faded; no one else existed. It was just the two of us.

> *Heal me, O Lord, and I shall be healed; save me, and I shall be saved: for thou art my praise. – Jeremiah 17:14*

That day the Lord healed my heart. Nothing the church members or pastor did or said affected me anymore. The Lord healed the pain in me. I became stronger, started praying again, finding my way to ministry again, and refocusing on helping children.

Because of my experience with getting help from organizations like Feed the Children, I had a long-standing desire to help other children. I wanted to do something for them when I got older and had the financial means to do so. I always wanted to give back and make a safe home for children in Uganda who were like my siblings and me. My mom and I wanted to start a home for orphans. She was extremely supportive and had the same heart of compassion, so we planned that she would lead the organization we would create to help orphans in Uganda. We looked at the architecture with her desire for a compound where children could play and have birthday parties, etc., in mind.

In 2005, I had a vision that God wanted me to start helping children. At the time, God was using my mom to help me. I didn't know she was never going to see the vision come to pass. I didn't know how to start a children's home; I didn't have money. I had a job, but it wasn't bringing in a lot of money. But God said, "I will send the people to stand with you and help you; all I want you to do is to start." So I started with my mom's help. People gave clothes, shoes, etc., and we took them to slums where children really needed help.

On one such occasion, I met a girl called Jane. She was severely poor. Every Christmas, my mom, siblings, and I would collect things from people and distribute them at Jane's church. I also would split my salary with them. Jane was a little girl who was underage yet working as a housemaid. Her story was heartbreaking. Her mother had gone insane, and I don't know what happened to her father. But he was not in the picture. So somebody brought her to the city to work as a housemaid. The family she worked for allowed her to come to church when she had finished her chores. Still, Jane had never worn shoes in her life.

So on this particular Christmas Eve, I had come back to Uganda from Switzerland (I was already married). We collected donations, toys, and other things from Switzerland and brought them to Jane's church. However, the highlight was when we gave Jane a pair of shoes. She was thirteen or fourteen years old and didn't know how a person walked with shoes. She could not believe she had her own pair of shoes. She walked like a baby trying to balance and walk with shoes for the first time. It was very emotional for me because I had a connection with her. She said to the pastor of the church, "Look, pastor. I have shoes, I have shoes!"

I will never forget the feeling I had watching Jane trying to walk in shoes for the first time in her life. It gave me more confidence to do the work and complete the children's home. So I continued forward. If God puts a vision in your heart, he can provide what's needed to fulfill it. He said, "I will provide; you just have to start." Sometimes he just wants you to use what is in your hand. All I had to do was be obedient. I started, I was obedient, and now I wasn't alone in the vision anymore. My husband had joined me. We started sharing what we were doing for Ugandan children with people in Switzerland, and support grew.

Things were getting better, but I didn't know the gross challenge that would soon come. That year my mother got extremely sick. She was struggling with stomach ulcers and blood pressure, and her heart had never been strong. While in Switzerland, I got a call that mommy was not well, and I had to go home to Uganda. Before my return, a miracle happened. Someone gave us a donation to construct the children's home. It was amazing; I was so excited. I went home, mommy got better, and we started the home for children.

But there was a devastating turn; my mom passed away one and a half months after I returned to Uganda. I had been with my mom during her time of sickness before she passed away. God used me to help my mom, to escort and prepare her to transition to glory. I didn't know that God was going to take my mother. In her heart, she was ready to go because she had a relationship with the Lord. But I was determined that God was going to heal my mother, but she wanted to go. So mommy rested in the Lord, and I was heartbroken. When a parent dies, it feels as if there's a piece of you that disappears with them. Two weeks after she passed, we found the house for the children. It was exactly how she wanted it, and we bought it with the money we had gotten from the donation.

I returned to Switzerland, but I was still struggling with losing my mom. For so long, I asked God why he didn't show up when I needed him the most. When something like that happens, people often have a lot of questions. I asked God, where were you? Why didn't you come? I went through dark times. Because I watched her die, I had nightmares. I would wrestle with the nightmares during the night and sleep through the day in response to the weariness, grief, and pain. I regularly cried myself to sleep because of the memory of watching her die.

Even worse, she died shortly before my birthday. So I didn't want to celebrate my birthday. I was still grieving.

But my mother-in-law called and said she wanted to cook dinner and bake a cake for me. I told her there's nothing to celebrate. She told me I would love to do something for you; you don't have to be alone. This is what your mother would want. My mother and mother-in-law always liked each other and cared about each other. It was a blessing for me to have in-laws that accepted my family and me. They never got a chance to meet each other in person, but they always spoke on the phone and liked each other.

So my husband said, "Let's go to my parents' place. It will be nice for you to get out of the house." I agreed to go but made it clear that I was not in a party mood. I told him we'll just go, have dinner, and come back home.

While driving to his parents' house, my husband said, "You have to talk to him." I hadn't been talking to God. I was so angry and sad. My husband said, "Talk to him. You have to talk to him. Tell him how you feel." And I said no. I felt that if I opened up and talked to God, all the anger, emotions, and everything I felt would come out. I knew he was going to start dealing with it and love on me. But I just wanted to stay angry. I knew God would start talking to me and embrace me, and I didn't want that—I wanted to stay angry.

After returning home from his parents' house, for the first time in months, that evening, I stayed up, came to the sitting room, and opened my mouth to talk to God. The first thing I said was, "Where were you?" I was really upset. I started to yell. I just yelled, "Where were you; how could you have not been there when I needed you? How could you let me down? Why didn't you do something?"

Sometimes God lets us get it all out because he wants to heal, cuddle, and speak to us. But because we are so much in our mourning and sadness, we carry everything on top of our shoulders and leave him out.

I cried and fell to the ground. It was as if Jesus walked into the room, and I could feel his presence. He put his hand on me, and I cried. It was like all the emotions and pain I had been carrying came out, and I wept bitterly. My husband was awake in the bedroom, but he did not try to come out or intervene. He knew it was between God and me, and I needed that time. I audibly heard Jesus say, "I never left Lydia. I never left. I was there the whole time. I tried to talk to you, but you did not listen. But I never left."

Suddenly, I felt this lightness and clarity coming to my heart, and this dark cloud just left me. And I said, "But how were you there?" He took me back a few weeks before my mother died. Some friends of ours were praying for my mom at the hospital. While praying, someone had a vision of my mother and me. I was escorting my mom in a canoe on a lake. Then we got to a certain place where I had to stay on the side, and she continued and crossed over to the other side where people were waiting for her with lights. But I did not think much of it at that time.

Another person saw a vision of my mom in a room with fragile glasses, and she was like an elephant. In this room, everything was so easily breakable that she didn't have room to move. She didn't have space to move, and Jesus came and broke her out of this room, so she was free and had space to move. So God said, "I tried to tell you and prepare you, but you were so focused on one thing—your mom being healed. I tried to tell you it was time for me to take her. She was ready to go, and this was between her and me." I wish I had listened; I wish I had paid attention to what God was saying. It would have still been painful to lose her. But I wouldn't have gone through the dark time, depression, anxiety, and pain. So I told God, "I'm sorry that I didn't listen, and I wanted my will to be done and not your will." Healing and peace came that night.

*Precious in the sight of the Lord is the death of his saints. – Psalm 116:15*

# Chapter 12: Birthing: Ministry And Children

*Her children arise up, and call her blessed; her husband also, and he praiseth her. – Prov. 31: 28*

After mom died, I had said I would never go back to Uganda. I wanted to sell the house and give back the donation money we received for the children's home. I wanted to close the door because of the pain of losing my mom. But that night, God brought back the passion for continuing the work we had started. In honor of my mom, we registered the children's home. We called it Home of Hope and Joy Again Foundation because God gave me back hope and joy when I didn't have hope for this project or joy to do it anymore. And my mother's name happened to be Joyce, and people used to call her Joy, so the name was simply perfect. And that's how the children's ministry was born. We didn't want to call it an orphanage because I feel the word orphanage is too final.

My siblings, husband, and I worked together to set up House of Hope and Joy Again. We bought everything and prepared the house, including beds, mattresses, and other things, thinking it would be a home for children we did not know. We set up the home, and it was running, and everything was okay. My husband, siblings, and I have continued the work, and it has been ten years now. The work is thriving and moving forward.

Five years went by, and we were helping some of the neediest children in the area. God had healed me of the grief I experienced after losing my mom. But now, I would have to face another loss. None of us thought that our sister would die unexpectedly. Grace was my big sister; we were the two girls in the family.

And she had eight children she was leaving behind—yes, eight. The youngest was only six months old when she passed away. I would send Grace money from time to time, but she worked. She was a single parent with no help from the children's father.

Before she passed away, I spoke to her one day, and she said she was feeling sick. I encouraged her to go to the hospital. She kept saying I went, they told me this, they told me that, and on and on. But my sister lived in the countryside, and never went to the city doctors, which was a bad mistake. I feel that if she had gone to a better doctor, she might have gotten better help and recovered.

The doctor she saw misdiagnosed her and gave her the wrong medication, which led to organ failure. Her liver failed, and by the time I got a phone call from my niece, my sister was already in a coma in a city hospital. She fell into a coma for three days and never woke up. She had tried to call me some days before, but I saw her missed call and said to myself that I would call her back. But the next day, before I could call her back, my niece called with the news that Grace was in a coma. I never got to say goodbye or tell my sister that I loved her. I never got the chance to be by her side like I had been with mommy when she passed away.

She died unexpectedly as a single parent; the children's father was not involved. So we had no choice but to step in and take care of my sister's children. We already had this home we were setting up. There was no way my brothers and I could see our sister's children suffer and not do anything. God had given me the grace to love other children, and these were my nieces and nephews. So how much more love was I to show them.

It was 2014 when I lost my big sister. Her name, Grace Safinah Biru, means beautiful. I miss her every day. We share the same birth month. My birthday is November 22nd, and her birthday is November 23rd. Each time she called on my birthday, she would sing a funny song to me. "Happy birthday to you. You look like a monkey." It was a funny thing just between us. Living far away from each other, we never ended a call without saying, "I love you. I hope you know how much I love you, and I miss you."

One time she told me, "You know I'm having all these kids for you." My husband would say, "Oh, no, no, no, no, no you're not!" It was weird. It was like a joke, but now, I remind my husband that she said she was having all the kids for us. Now we have ten children (only two are our biological children), and we love them all.

My big sister gave me the gift of being a mom to such amazing nieces and nephews. They don't call me aunty. They call me mommy. Most of them are taller than me; I look up into their eyes and give them guidance. And they are all born-again believers. How amazing! They serve the Lord. God has helped me to walk with them and teach them about the Lord. They are growing in Jesus, and that's awesome to me. I think any parent would be incredibly pleased to have all their children loving the Lord. They all are thriving in different ways.

So my sister birthed children but also helped to birth me into motherhood. After she passed away, God continued to work in my life. I not only birthed a ministry but also my own biological children.

In addition to working with the children's home, I started preaching online. I developed an online church via Skype before social media platforms like Facebook, Instagram, and Twitter had "live" options. We were meeting once a week with people from different countries like Japan, Sweden, Denmark, Switzerland, and Uganda. The Lord started opening doors for me to minister in various conferences and travel the world.

By that time, I was praying about finding a local church in Switzerland. I was asking God where I should go, which church. There was a conference going on nearby, and my husband said, let's go. There was a guest speaker from the United States. We went to the conference, and it was something I had missed for a long time. The Lord was there; the speaker prophesied and ministered powerfully.

I continued to preach via Skype. As I continued to pray about which church to join, I would see the face of the pastor of the church that held the conference. I told my husband, and he agreed, so I joined that church. They welcomed us with open arms. It was the first church I went to in Switzerland that didn't make me feel like a foreigner. They were happy to have us and embraced us even though we were a mixed couple.

After that, my husband and I were blessed with our second child, a son. We had prayed, and people had given us prophecies about us having a child. It was a miraculous birth, and we were so grateful to God for the blessing of our son. Our first son was born in 2013, and our second son in 2018.

After our first son was born, I got an invitation to minister in Japan, and it was such a fruitful trip. We took our first son with us. God touched his people and showed himself strong. While there, we were on the street looking for a restaurant. We didn't have a translator with us; we had left all our friends back at the place where we were staying. But we prayed for the Lord to lead us and used our mobile phones to translate as best as possible.

We saw a restaurant called *Afro Restaurant*. We thought it was an African restaurant based on the name, but they didn't even sell African food. They were wearing Afro wigs. So, of course, we were a bit surprised. We asked the Lord if it was where he wanted us to go. So my husband, son, and I walked into the restaurant.

They were not used to seeing an actual African person, and my son has an afro (big hair), and it's not a wig. They were all wearing these wigs. It was quite a sight; Japanese people wearing Afro wigs! Also, we had to use our mobile phones to translate and try to understand each other. They reacted, saying, "Oh my God, can I touch your hair? Can we take pictures with you? We agreed.

We had dinner, and then the Lord started to speak to me about the restaurant owner. I asked him some questions and spoke into his life prophetically. He started crying and told us all the things I was saying were true. He gave his life to the Lord. One of the customers was so touched that he wanted to pay for our food. They joined tables together, and we were singing and dancing and having a good time together. It was amazing. I still have contact with the young man who got born again.

Never be afraid to go where the Lord wants you to go. Even if there's a language barrier, he will still use you if you are in the right place. So the Lord was always there to carry me through and show me the way. I think of God as my belt, the belt that holds me together because, without him, I would not be here.

When we brought our first child to Japan with us—he was two years old. We wanted a second child and started praying about it.

# Chapter 13: Our God Reigns

We continued praying for a second child. The pastors in our new local church were supportive and stood with us. We had been happy, and people had been asking when we would have another child. But it was difficult. I had two miscarriages. The first was four years after our first son was born. During the miscarriage, the doctors told us we had to wait until the bleeding stopped before they could do anything to help me. I was having terrible cramps and pains, but they couldn't give me strong medication because sometimes some pregnancies do bleed. They told me the baby might still survive, so they couldn't do much. We had to wait.

Going through a miscarriage is a very devasting and painful thing. Post-partum depression is very real, and so much more is the depression that can attack you when you lose a child. Some people suffer severely. They don't want to talk and blame themselves for losing their baby. It was difficult to open up to the people closest to me. The women in my family didn't understand. They said I didn't have to talk about it; I should get over it because it wasn't like I gave birth to a baby. They had no idea of the emotional challenges I was experiencing.

After the miscarriage, we were praying at home and had put on worship music, and I had a vision of the words "God Reigns" written on our wall. I told my husband that I had seen this picture of the words "God Reigns." I knew that I had lost the pregnancy. Somehow, he gave me peace.

I had this picture of me, Jesus, and the baby at the beach. But the miscarried child was with Jesus. He said he would give us more children. I shared this with my husband.

I got pregnant two months later. And again, we had another miscarriage. I told the Lord that I would not accept falling into depression because I knew some women never recovered from such a thing. I asked the Lord to protect me and not let me fall into a dark hole of depression. Some people told us to quit trying, accept fate, and that we would only have one child. Some said I was too old, but I was just thirty-two. My husband was resolved that if God promised us children, he would fulfill his promise. He told me that we were not going to listen to people's negativity but would trust and believe in God.

When people are saying contradictory things, you must hold on to the word of God. It's important to read the word of God. That is the truth. Only the word of God is telling the truth. He said in his word, I will bless you and bless the fruit of your womb. We chose to focus on that word and believe him. God reigns, whether in difficulty or good times. I was pregnant three times in the same year.

A few months before the birth of our second child, I used to have dreams where I would see myself in the hospital having a baby and bleeding a lot. I kept having this feeling that I would have the baby and he would be fine, but something would happen to me. I felt it. I called my brothers and told them about these dreams that I kept having. We prayed together against it with my family and my pastors. It was like God was communicating to us about what was going to happen to me.

In October of 2017, I declared, "Lord, you're going to give us a Christmas miracle." I took a pregnancy test in November, and it was positive. I invited our families over for dinner during Christmas and told them we were pregnant (about two months after the declaration). Our families were so happy and gave us advice to take it easy and stay on bed rest. Everyone had advice to give. All the people who were naysayers joined in celebrating with us, saying, "We knew it would happen." But the Lord is always faithful to those who wait on him. Those who call upon his name will not be put to shame. All those who had been against it came together and celebrated with us.

We entered 2018 pregnant, waiting for a beautiful baby boy who was born in July. He came three weeks early in July. It was a quick birth; five hours in labor, and he was out.

> *When the LORD turned again the captivity of Zion, we were like them that dream. – Psalm 126:1*

Ten minutes after I gave birth, the doctor had a certain look on her face. I was holding the baby, and my husband was next to me on the bed. I asked her if everything was okay. She told me I was bleeding too much, but they were trying to handle it. The next minute, she asked my husband to please take the baby from me.

Now she had a serious look on her face. Then, she pressed the emergency button, and more people start storming into the room one by one. She told my husband to please step out of the room with the baby. He was confused and asked what was going on, but they told him they had no time to explain; they needed to work on his wife. Suddenly, I felt as if I was going to faint.

"Oh no, hold her neck. Don't let her bite her tongue," the doctor said. I was feeling weaker and weaker. All the doctors who had worked on me were called back to the room to explain what they had done and the medications they had given me. There were ten or so doctors in the room. "You're bleeding too much; you're bleeding out, and we don't know exactly where it is coming from," they said. They told me they were trying to stop the bleeding, but it was too much, and they didn't even know where it was coming from.

Two nurses were pressing my stomach and pulling and pulling. Another nurse was pressing my neck, trying to find arteries. I looked down and saw the doctor put something like a plastic balloon into my uterus. My uterus spat out the balloon, and blood dashed out. My blood pressure went so low I started feeling very cold; I was freezing, shivering, and in and out of consciousness. I asked if someone could cover me.

They told me they were doing everything they could, and I just started to pray in tongues. I told the Lord, "You are the doctor now; I need you to do something." I felt the presence of God. I didn't have any fear anymore. I knew God was in the room and was fighting for me.

The doctors were running up and down. They put something in me like a big spoon to scrub out the blood, but nothing was working. I had the baby at 3 a.m.; I started bleeding out at 3:10 a.m. Three hours later, they were still trying to stop the bleeding. They were putting blood directly in my arteries and doing whatever they thought would help.

My husband was waiting outside with the baby, and the baby was still naked in a towel. He saw people running back and forth. The lead doctor said, "What do we do now because we're losing her." Someone said, "Let's call the surgeon. Maybe there's something they can do—something we haven't been able to do." So she called and put the phone on speaker. She told them, "I have a patient here; it's been three hours. We've been trying to stop the bleeding, and it's not working. What can you guys do?" The phone was on speaker, so I could hear everything he was saying. He told her, "Sorry, at the moment we are busy. We have a lady who is delivering right now." So the doctor asked again, "What do you want us to do? My patient is dying; she's bleeding out." The guy just hung up the phone. She started beating the phone on the table because she was so upset.

I was shivering and in and out of consciousness. They kept putting things to my nose to keep me from falling asleep. "Stay awake; we don't want you to fall into a coma," they said. One doctor said, "Let's call the hospital chief." That was around 6 a.m. They called the chief. He came quickly and asked, "What's going on? They explained. He started asking so many questions. What did you do? How much medicine did you give her? She told him they had called the surgeon, and he did nothing. He called the surgeon back and told him if this woman dies, we're all responsible. "I don't want to hear any excuses; this is a command. You must do something now," he barked. It was a scene straight out of Grey's Anatomy.

So they brought me out; there was a nurse on top of me on the bed pressing down on my stomach and another on the side pressing the oxygen. They rolled me out; they stopped very quickly outside to brief my husband. He was still holding the baby. They told him I was bleeding out, and there were two options. Either they would take my uterus or do an embolization, which is like a heart bypass but for the uterus. I removed the oxygen mask and said, "What! You want to remove my uterus. First of all, I want to have more kids. But right now, please just save me without taking out my uterus." They told my husband it was serious and to say goodbye to me. He put the baby on me, and the baby was crying, and my husband was crying. I whispered to him, "Don't forget my kids in Uganda. Take care of the kids."

I don't know how I was so strong. I was not panicking. It was like someone was holding me up. And the doctors were asking me how is it that you are so strong, why are you not panicking. I said, "He's here." I could feel and sense the Lord in the room, but they couldn't. So they thought maybe I was tripping. I asked if someone could pray with me. The doctor said, "My faith right now is zero. I can't even focus to pray, but I'm doing everything I can to save you." So I just kept on praying and worshipping.

They rolled me to the theater. Everyone was on standby. The surgeon told me he wanted me to play dead for him. They would move me. "You just breathe; don't move," he said. Even just to roll on my side, they moved me. They put me between these two machines, and he had to do the embolization. He needed two hours.

Using the camera, he went in with the catheter and made an incision. He went in very slow and put in medicine to cut off the blood supply to the uterus to stop the bleeding. It took about two hours but thank God, it worked.

I had been unconscious for about two hours. After coming back to consciousness, I could see that it was daytime; it was bright. When I opened my eyes, they asked me if I had any pain and whether I needed anything. I asked them if my husband knew where I was and if anyone was telling him what's going on with me. They said yes, someone is with him. The baby is fine; he's breathing on his own. The baby had come early but was doing fine. So they asked me again if I needed anything, and I told them I just wanted to go home.

But they put me in the Intensive Care Unit (ICU). I was hooked on so many machines, and that place was so dark. There was a male patient next to me who was crying, screaming, and yelling. I don't know what he had, but he was just screaming. It was so sad. People who had patients there in the ICU all walked with a heavy demeanor. It was scary to be there. I had two doctors and several nurses working around the clock on me. I had all these catheters and things connected to me. I wasn't allowed to be moved, and they were worried that my organs might fail.

After almost seven hours, I was able to see my baby and really have time to hold him and see my husband. My husband was able to come in briefly with the baby. He called my family, and everyone was on standby. When they were rushing me to surgery, I had forgotten to tell him to tell people to pray, but I had left my phone with him. So he went through my phone and texted anyone he knew was a believer and asked them to pray. He had called my brothers and told them, and they put up a chain of prayer. It was early in the morning. He called my brothers again when I was out of surgery. I spoke to my younger brother first, and he said, "Lynn, are you okay?" I said yes, and he just burst out in tears, saying, "You almost gave me a heart attack. Don't do this again! No more babies."

All I can say is the Lord is so great. My body healed so fast; it was supernatural. That evening I could move to a normal room even though I had lost three and a half liters of blood.

If I had been in a hospital where they could not perform that surgery, I would be dead today. Indeed, in our area, it was only in that hospital that you could find the machine the surgeon needed to do the embolization. And the surgeon who performed the surgery had only five minutes to end his shift when they called and stopped him from going home. God is amazing!

I spent only five days in the hospital after giving birth. We had a family suite. We paid only for three days, and the hospital gave the rest to us for free. So my husband could stay and help me with the baby because I couldn't carry anything. But when I went home, it was like nothing had ever happened. I gave birth on Monday, and on Saturday, I went home. Our Christmas miracle manifested in July of 2018 despite my almost bleeding to death. We gave him the middle name Reign because God reigns—always!

> *The LORD shall reign forever, even thy God, O Zion, unto all generations. Praise ye the LORD. – Psalm 146:10*

# Section 5: Ministry

# Chapter 14: Present Day: The Miracles Continue

> *But ye shall receive power, after that the Holy Ghost is come upon you: and ye shall be witnesses unto me both in Jerusalem, and in all Judaea, and in Samaria, and unto the uttermost part of the earth.*
> *– Acts 1:8*

It was a privilege to take our first son to Japan. God had richly blessed us with the fruit of the womb, miraculously rescued me, and again strengthened our faith in him. We continued to travel for conferences in various nations. We saw so many miracles, signs, wonders, and doors being opened for the sake of the gospel.

My husband confronted his old pastor about all the things he had done to us and told him he was leaving the church and joining me in ministry full-time. The pastor still refused to acknowledge that he did anything wrong. We were both ordained together and now serve God together as a couple.

As we launched out together, through Facebook (ministering online), we got to know a young man who was a doctor. He had gotten a job offer to work with the United Nations in Somalia. This doctor and one of his good friends were both given job offers with the United Nations. But before accepting, he contacted me and asked me to pray for him. He requested that I ask the Lord if he should take the job. I prayed, and the Lord said to tell him not to go because he would be killed. God also said that he would provide for him and compensate him if he didn't go. I told him what the Lord said in prayer, and he was so sad. He called his friend to let him know he would not be accepting the job offer. His friend accepted the job and went anyway. However, a week later, his friend's convoy was attacked in Somalia. His friend, along with everyone else with him, was killed. Through prayer, God had warned this young doctor. Thank God he listened and did not go.

He was really shaken and shocked by the death of his friend. But after that, the Lord gave him a job with the American Embassy. God compensated him as he had promised. The American Embassy gave him a five-year contract. But after two years, he wanted to go to the United Kingdom (UK). So he left the job with the American Embassy to relocate to the UK. They paid out his pension fund, which helped him travel, get settled in the UK, and get more professional licenses there. He later married and is now living in the UK with his family and working as a more highly credentialed doctor. We initially met online but physically in person for the first time in 2019. The Lord rescued him and compensated him for obedience.

In 2019, we were twice in England to minister at conferences, and we are now an independent ministry, Trinity's Love Ministries International (trinityslove.org). We work with people from all over the globe, and the Lord has been good. He has been amazing and is still amazing.

In 2019, we also went back to Uganda for the first time in eight years. My sons got to meet their Ugandan family for the first time. It was a surprise because they didn't know we were coming.

We just had a conference recently where God healed a man who had a heart attack two months prior to the conference. The doctors made a mistake during the operation, and he lost feeling and senses in his genitals (private parts). Early in the morning on the first day of the conference, the Lord woke me up and told me a man was coming to the conference that had a problem with his private parts and he would heal him. I didn't know how to say it at the conference. My translator did not want to face the congregation to say it. It was initially uncomfortable to address.

So I said, "What I'm about to say may be uncomfortable, but I'm going to obey the Holy Spirit and say it." For a moment, there was silence. I said, "You don't have to come to the front; we can pray for you in private." Suddenly, a grown man jumped up and said it was him who was having the problem. "I have a testimony to give," he said. "While you were talking about my condition, I felt like a sharp cut, and I want to tell you my private parts are alive and functioning." There was such relief in my heart! When you speak that kind of thing, you are praying to God that you have not missed it and that someone comes forward.

But there is no situation that is too hard for God. I did not touch this man to pray for him. Because of the COVID-19 rules at that time, we were not allowed to touch anyone. God touched him. By the time we finished the three-day conference, he was dancing. He said, "I feel nothing! God gave me a new heart. Everything is new." Brothers and sisters, this is why we do what we do. This is what ministry is all about—changing lives. This is how we ended 2020. There's never a dull moment with the Lord. So I encourage you to know him and serve him.

There's always a way for those who trust and depend on the Lord. He always has a plan for each of us. He's loving and forgiving, always ready to give us another chance. Every day there's mercy to start over. So if you want to give up and think God has disappointed you, or you see no way out, take a deep breath and talk to him. He's always ready to listen, forgive, and give you a new chance.

My life and the stories I've shared with you are a testimony to this truth. God supernaturally provided for us in severe poverty. He rescued me from the point of suicide, healed my body after seven years of sickness, healed my heart when my husband's church was coming against me, and spoke to me after losing my mom. He's a loving heavenly Father that I can say with full assurance is real. And because of that, I want you to consider an essential decision and prayer.

## *An Essential Decision and Prayer*

If Jesus showed up at your door and asked if he could come into your house, would you tell him to let you first clean up before he came in? But if you would just open your heart and say come in, then this prayer is for you. If you're ready to give God a chance to show you how real he is, just say the following prayer. It's short and simple but everlasting.

Dear Lord Jesus, I am a sinner. Forgive me of my sins. Come into my heart and change me. Cleanse me with your precious blood. Write my name in the book of life. Today, I accept you as my Lord and personal savior. Fill me with your Holy Spirit and baptize me. In the name of the Father, Son, and the Holy Spirit, I pray. Amen.

# About the Author

Pastor Lydia Bohi was born and raised in Kampala Uganda. She is a wife, mother, author, former nursing aid, and minister of the gospel. She is the founder of Hope and Joy Again foundation, a children's home based in Uganda, which focuses on giving young people a home and safe place to stay while teaching them about Jesus. Together with her husband, they are the senior pastors of Trinity's Love Ministries International based in Switzerland.

www.ingramcontent.com/pod-product-compliance
Lightning Source LLC
Chambersburg PA
CBHW071702040426
42446CB00011B/1870